# Dirt Busters

*Revised edition*

Library of Congress Catalog Card Number: 91-66362

ISBN 0-9621757-0-6

Cover design by Kari Allen and George Riemann
Layout by Robert Shaw


Published by:
Peters and Thornton Publishers
3483 Golden Gate Way
Lafayette, California  94549


Printed in the United States of America

# *Dirt Busters*

by
Margaret Dasso
Maryan Skelly

Peters and Thornton Publishers
Lafayette, California

# Table of Contents

*The problem with doing housework is that nobody notices. The problem with not doing housework is that everybody notices.*

*Anonymous*

# 1

## *Just Like Mom Used to Do*

**L**et's face it: Housework is a fact of life! Somebody's got to do it, and if that "body" is you, chances are you'd like to do it as quickly and easily as possible. Unfortunately, few of us have ever had the opportunity to learn how to clean efficiently—in fact most haven't even given it much thought.

It's like the story—supposedly true—about the woman who always cut the end off a ham before cooking it. Why? "Because that's the way you're supposed to do it; Mother always did." Come to find out, Mother always cut the end off because she never had a pan big enough to accommodate a whole ham!

If we stop and think about it there are a lot of things we do because "Mother always did"—and they're probably just as foolish. And why did Mother always do it that way? Because her Mother did! We'd like to offer you a better way.

*Woman's Work! Housework's the hardest work in the world. That's why men won't do it*

*Edna Ferber*

# 2

## Learning to Do It Right

**B**ack in 1980, when our housekeeping agency, The Clean Sweep, was still just a dream, we realized that being born female in no way ensures that a person knows how to clean efficiently or well (we knew this from firsthand experience). If we were to have the very best possible staff, we would have to research efficient cleaning techniques. We wanted a simple "paint by numbers" manual that would show anyone how to clean in a professional manner.

With sharpened pencils and yellow legal pads in hand, we descended upon the main library, there to immerse ourselves in the latest in housekeeping technology and techniques. We were prepared to seek and record THE TRUTH. You'd think we were researching ancient Sanskrit greeting cards, there was so little information on the subject. This was startling. After all, over half of the adult population is involved with housework at some level, and most of these people would rather do just about anything else. Furthermore, there are how-to books on every conceivable subject. Why not housecleaning?

Undaunted, we turned to friends who had majored in home economics in college. It seemed logical that if they had spent precious college time learning how to sew on a button properly, they surely would have

3

learned how to clean a house efficiently. They checked their textbooks and talked with friends in the field. This netted us a few ideas but we were still a long way from a manual of any substance.

It was at this point that Margaret's husband's second cousin by marriage dropped in from the sky. Coincidentally, she and another woman had been cleaning houses for a couple of years. She not only knew *what* she was doing but *why*. She had experimented with various procedures, continually refining her techniques. She provided us with a wealth of information. Interviews with other professional housekeepers followed.

Now we were getting somewhere.

After more searching and researching, talking and testing, writing and rewriting, we finally had our manual. A manual to offer to all prospective housekeepers in our yet-to-be-realized company.

## Some Practical Experience

Before placing the manual in anyone's hands, ihowever, it seemed necessary to test the procedures therein. (After all, our husbands scoffed heartily at the mere mention that we could teach others how to clean.) And so it was that we set about to clean for a few generous friends who were helping us launch our new business.

We were astonished at how much more we could accomplish by using our new found procedures. "Efficiency is the key," we declared. And though it may sound boring--bringing to mind, as it does, slightly balding, bespectacled men, long of neck and narrow of shoulder, pursing their lips as they record time/motion data on charts and graphs--efficiency means you can accomplish more work in less time. Efficiency means you are out of the kitchen and into the family room, picnic area, shopping mall, bubble bath, committee meeting or wherever else you'd like to be. Efficiency buys you extra hours in your day.

## We're Still Learning

Since those early days, we've worked with several hundred housekeepers and done well over 80,000 housecleanings. We've learned a lot from housekeepers and clients alike and we changed our manual accordingly. Its effectiveness has been proven over and over. We hope you find this information as helpful as our housekeepers have through the years.

But first, a word about cleaning supplies. (Sounds dreadfully dull, we know, but proper "tools" can make all the difference in how much time and effort you need to invest in cleaning.)

*No one knows what a (housewife's) life expectancy is, but I have a horror of leaving this world and not having anyone in the entire family know how to replace the toilet tissue spindle.*

Erma Bombeck
**If Life is a Bowl of Cherries, Why am I in the Pits?**

# 3

## Cleaning Your Home Dirt Cheap

You may be spending too much on cleaning supplies! On the other hand, you may need to add to or upgrade your existing tools (equipment). We believe you should pare down both to just a few essentials. There's no reason to buy one of everything on the supermarket shelf when just a few supplies will do; and bargain brands are often just as effective as those high-priced products touted on television. With the money you save you can buy a few pieces of high-quality equipment. You wouldn't expect a carpenter to use a $2.98 hammer would you? You need good tools too!

You can easily save yourself $150 or more per year and many trips to the grocery store if you will buy your cleaning supplies at a janitorial supply house or discount warehouse outlet. The products generally come in gallon jugs and are highly concentrated. You can also buy sponges, mops, dust cloths–virtually everything you need. One trip a year should suffice.

Since you may wish to continue to use products from the grocery or hardware store, those are the ones we've listed here.

## Essential Supplies

**All Purpose Cleaner** (*409, Fantastik*, etc.)–Despite the extravagant claims, one works as well as another. But experiment. You may find you have a preference. Also consider these alternatives:

- Sudsy ammonia and hot water. Many people swear by this, and it will certainly save you money.
- There is also a new ammonia by *Parsons* especially formulated for windows. This can be used to clean just about anything in the house. A real time saver.
- A new product called *Now* is available at some discount warehouse stores. At about $9 per gallon, this highly concentrated cleaner will really save you money. In addition, it's environmentally safe. So you can mop the floor with it, then empty the bucket in your rose bed (a real boon to us Californians.)

*Clean Earth* is an all purpose cleaner we tested because a) it is "eco friendly" and b) it was on the supermarket shelf. But it turned out to be the best cleaner we've ever used. Surprisingly, you don't even have to wait for it to set up. Even the toughest grease and grime comes off with one swipe. If your supermarket doesn't carry *Clean Earth*, write to them at: Clean Earth, Cabot Cosmos Corp., 570 West Lambert Rd., Suite L, Brea, CA 92621, or call (714) 990-1983.

**Glass Cleaner**–Any commercial product is fine, or make your own (see chapter 7).

**Paper Towels**–*Microwave Bounty* is the best we've tested. Bargain brands are no bargain for cleaning.

**Rags and/or Sponges**–Some people like one, others use both. If you use rags, be sure they are absorbent. This is not the place for old undershirts. For best results, buy a yard or so of linen, cut it into pieces about 18" square, and hem the edges. Cloth baby diapers are also terrific. Old terry cloth toweling ranks "next best." Regarding sponges: Buy good quality cellulose or natural. One should be as large as you can handle comfortably for big jobs like floors or kitchen counters; another should be smaller for tighter areas. You may also like one that has the plastic scrubbing surface on one side.

**Dust Cloth**–Buy a treated one or make one out of old nylon stockings or squares of pure cotton or wool fabric. The materials build up static electricity which attracts the dust.

**Toothbrush**–An old one is fine, just be sure it has flat bristles and a straight handle.

**Plastic Scrubber Pad**–Any brand that's safe for Teflon is okay, but *Dobie* is generally the easiest to use.

**Cleaning Caddy**–helpful for carrying supplies from room to room. You can use a bucket, but then you have to take everything out when you want to use it. A caddy is worth the couple of dollars it will cost you. Your hardware store should carry them. Some people just keep cleaning supplies in each room. That's great for touch-up cleaning, but why spend all the extra time getting them out and then putting them away? It doesn't make sense.

**Upright Vacuum** (plus extra bags, fan belt and extension cord)--More is not necessarily better here. In fact, some of the most expensive vacuums are the most difficult to use. The features to look for are a motor of at least 6 amps, metal handles rather than plastic, top-fill disposable bags and an effective beater bar.

All the dealers we talked to agree that *The Boss* by Eureka is the best all-around vacuum for the money. At this writing, it sells for somewhere between $100-129.

Don't waste your money on extra attachments. Buy a mini-vac instead.

**Mini-Vac** (a small, carry around canister vacuum)–Eureka's *Mighty Mite*--(often on sale for $70 or $120 depending on horsepower) or Panasonic are the best for our money. Once you use one, you'll wonder how you ever managed without it.

OR...

**Combination-Type Vacuum**–A long hose attaches a power head to the canister, giving you some of the best features of an upright and mini- vac. If this vacuum interests you, be sure to give it a good workout at the store. Some people feel it's like pulling a ball and chain around with them, while other people wouldn't have any other type of vacuum. If you choose this type, be sure the power head is equipped with a beater bar for your carpets.

## Optional Supplies

**Spray Bottles**–Good quality sprayers purchased from a janitorial supply house or hardware store can save you scads of time and frustration. Label them with a permanent felt marker and they will last for years.

**Concentrated All Purpose Cleaner**–Use for heavy-duty cleaning, such as soap scum in the bathroom and grease in the kitchen. *Simple Green* is probably the most popular around here, but there are a number of good ones. Also, remember ammonia and *Now*.

**Tub and Tile Cleaner**–The jury is still out on this one. Lots of people (including us) swear by *Shower Power* or others, yet consumer tests indicate an all purpose cleaner is just as effective. You be the judge.

**Disinfectant Cleaner**–Again, tests show that all purpose cleaners work just as well, but a disinfectant will kill some germs (although not as many as you might think) and it helps retard mildew. One brand is as good as another.

**Mildew Cleaner**–Buy a special one if you want, but a bleach/water solution works as well, and is a whole lot cheaper. *Clorox* recommends ³/₄ cup bleach to a gallon of water, but many people use a stronger solution. Be sure to rinse thoroughly.

**Powdered Cleanser**–Powdered or Liquid–Unless you have very old porcelain, or a stained toilet bowl, powdered cleanser is seldom necessary. Not only is it time-consuming to rinse off, it will abrade most any surface. (This is true, to a lesser degree, even for liquid cleansers, despite what the commercials may claim.)

**Toilet Brush**–The round, European type is ever so much better than the regular American variety. Try it.

**Dry Mop or Broom**–If you prefer a broom, buy the large size *O'Cedar* angled broom or similar one.

Don't waste your money on a great big cheap one. A mini-vac does the job of both.

**Wet Mop**–String or sponge-type, you choose. If you prefer a sponge mop, look for one by *Continental*. It has an extra large very durable sponge head that is slightly abrasive. Check your hardware or janitorial supply store. It is definitely worth a special trip.

The newest thing in mops enables you to clean not only floors, but walls, ceilings and windows as well, without a bucket! The secret is in removable terry cloth covers for the large (15x18"), ultra thin, swivel cleaning pad. You simply dampen the cover and slip it over the pad, changing the cover as necessary. Since it doubles as a dry mop, one piece of equipment takes the place of three. Ingenious!

This mop is not available in stores, but may be ordered through the Joan Cook Housewares catolog, 3200 S.E. 14th Avenue, Ft. Lauderdale, Fl 33350. The phone number is 1-800-327-3799. This is the premier catalog of its kind for product variety, prices and service.

**Bucket**–*Rubbermaid* makes a rectangular one that just barely fits the Continental mop (above). Choose a white or light colored bucket so you can tell when to change your rinse water. You may opt to use the sink rather than a bucket (see kitchen procedures).

**Rubber Gloves**–If you hate them, you've probably only tried the big floppy kind. Try the thin ones that come ten to a package and look like surgeons' gloves. They're available in hardware and some grocery stores. Or buy some *Platex Living Gloves* in the proper size. We see no evidence that they are truly a life form, but they fit great. Once you get used to rubber gloves, you'll love them–especially for those yikky jobs. (And if you apply a thick coat of hand cream before putting them on, your hands will look better after cleaning than before.)

**Furniture Polish**--Lemon oil works well, is inexpensive and has many other uses as well.

**Feather Duster**–Go for quality: lambswool or ostrich feather. If you have high ceilings, there are telescoping models.

*Dustbuster*–These are great for doing stairs, cupboard and drawer interiors, the fireplace hearth, and the like. There are a number of models to choose from: one has a rotating brush, another has attachments while some have more horsepower.

**Floor Care Products**–We don't need to tell you that there are a multitude of them on the market. Our only words of caution are: be sure you read directions carefully (some are tricky). And if you're going to apply any type of wax, be certain the floor is perfectly clean. There's nothing like ''gluing'' a hair to the floor with a coat of *Mop and Glo*.

**Apron**–The best style is either a cobbler apron or a smock with four pockets just below the waist. (If the pockets are too low, it is impractical to put your cleaners in them as they bang together too much as you move around.)

*Cleaning your house while your children
are still growing is like shoveling the
walk before it stops snowing.*

Phyllis Diller

# 4

# *The Truth as We Know It*

**O**kay, this is it. This is THE TRUTH as we know it. A culmination of ten years of research, observation and testing. Commit these principles to memory. Practice them. Once mastered, you will be amazed at your proficiency and efficiency. You will dazzle and amaze your friends, stupefy your family.

All right, all right, a bit of an exaggeration, perhaps. But one thing's for sure: anyone, yes, **ANYONE,** can master housework by using these fundamentals. Try them. You'll see.

**Work in an orderly manner**. You will accomplish far more in less time if you train yourself to work from left to right and top to bottom all the way around the room, doing the center of the room last. This means that you will clean everything you can while standing in one place.

Imagine you have paint on the soles of your shoes; every footstep is visible. When you have finished cleaning a room, there should be just one set of footprints all the way around the room, not a jumble of prints going this way and that. Never backtrack unless absolutely necessary. You can do it; you just have to be aware of what you're doing. Train yourself to be orderly.

**Keep your supplies close at hand**. All of your supplies will be in your cleaning caddy. Take out the ones you will need for the room you're working on and put them in your apron pocket. This way you won't need to carry the caddy with you while cleaning the room—a big timesaver.

**"If it ain't dirty, don't clean it!"** You may be surprised how much precious time you're spending cleaning things like an unused bathtub or the pictures in the living room just because they're there or because your mother always cleaned them every week. Unless you're a fanatic or have a lot of time on your hands, you don't need to clean everything every week! Not by a long shot. Experiment. Be aware. See how long you can go between dustings, for instance, before you hit your "dirt threshold." You might be surprised.

**Use only as much cleaning agent as is necessary.** Every extra squirt of window cleaner or all purpose cleaner translates into extra time to wipe it dry. This is especially important when washing mirrors, chrome, windows or shiny appliances. Try using less each time until you find the optimum amount. If this only saves you 30 wiping seconds per item, that's a 10 minutes saving. Can't you think of something you'd like to do for those 10 minutes?

**Don't Scrub!** It's an absolute waste of time and energy. Rather, let your cleaning agents work for you. Even plain water begins to break down the molecules of a surface the moment it touches it. When chemicals are added, the process is obviously that much faster. So whenever you have spots or general grime, apply cleaner to as large an area as practical, let it set up for as long as necessary and simply wipe or mop the area. Occasionally, you will need to use an abrasive pad (*Dobie,* etc.) to remove a stubborn spot, but you should never have to scrub. **CAUTION:** Never use this method on hardwood or vinyl square floors–the liquid could seep between the joints and damage the floor.

**Use a barely damp sponge on dry surfaces** whenever possible. If the surface is wet, you will have to dry it with a rag before cleaning it. If you don't you will dilute the cleaner by at least 50 percent.

**Read label directions on any new product.** You may be sure you know how and on what to use it, but you may be surprised. Remember, the experts have tested and retested the cleaner: learn from them.

If you're using something that needs to be diluted with water, keep in mind that more is not better. You'll cut the product's effectiveness whether you add too much or too little.

**Stop before you drop.** It's sometimes tempting to push yourself to work past your fatigue point. Although this may seem more efficient, it takes your body significantly longer to recover at this point. Two five minute breaks can refresh you, whereas you may still be exhausted after one 20-minute break. Work smart.

**Try to clean a little faster, a little more efficiently** each time. So much of your housework is merely routine–we've always done it this way or that. By simply being conscious of what, how and why you're doing things, you will probably devise all kinds of time and energy saving techniques. And you'll wonder why you "never thought of that before", when it is so obvious.

Sometimes even the smallest changes will reap significant rewards. Remember, every step, every movement you save pays off in greater speed and less fatigue.

*Isn't it nice that no one cares which twenty-three hours of the day I work?*

Thurgood Marshall

# 5

## *So–Let's Get Started!*

**W**e hope that our training manual, which follows, is useful to you either as a guide for your own cleaning routine or for a housekeeper you may hire. You may choose not to do all of these things each week–or ever! It all depends on your individual priorities, standards and, perhaps more importantly, the time and energy you have to devote to cleaning. Most of our customers find that they can get along with a thorough cleaning every other week and touch-ups in between.

If you are fortunate enough to have older children involved in the housework, you may want to put the procedure for each room on cards and tape them on the appropriate walls. This provides an impartial guide and can significantly improve the quality of work.

So grab your cleaning caddy, put on your apron and let's get started.

### Pre-Clean Routine

First check the upright vacuum cleaner bag. Put in

a new one if the contents are close to the middle. Check the mini-vac as well.

If the stove is electric, remove the drip pans and rims and soak them in a strong solution of dishwasher detergent (*Cascade, Electra-sol,* etc.).

Now move to the first room.


## The Bathroom Routine

❑ Remove **Throw Rugs**, if any, to the hall. Vacuum or shake them outside later.

❑ Remove hair from **Counters** and sink with vacuum cleaner attachment (if surface is dry) or a tissue. Do not use a sponge or rag.

❑ Spray **Tub, Tile and Glass Shower Doors** with all purpose cleaner. Let it set up if necessary.

Be sure to clean soap dish and all chrome in tub/shower area.

❑ Spray small amount of glass cleaner on **Mirror**. Wipe until absolutely dry. Check from an angle to be sure there are no streaks.

❑ Spray **Sink** with glass cleaner (or all purpose cleaner); wipe dry. Move items on vanity to one side, spray counter with glass cleaner. Move items back, wiping them as you go. Spray the remaining counter(s) and fixtures. Use a toothbrush around faucets and base of fixture. Wipe dry.

❑ To clean **Toilet**, spray all purpose cleaner on toilet brush and brush the bowl, starting under the rim and working around and down into throat of the bowl. Flush toilet.

Put toilet seat up, spray and wipe each side of seat

and lid. Spray and wipe tank, base and exposed pipes, using toothbrush as necessary.

Wipe toilet paper holder, using toothbrush if necessary.

❑ On your way **Around The Room,** wipe towel racks (using toothbrush if/where necessary), refold towels, dust pictures, shelves, etc.; check for fingerprints–especially on back of door and light switch cover.

❑ Wash **Floor.** Put rugs back after it dries.

## The Kitchen Routine

❑ Quickly check **Floor, Stove and Counters** for any stubborn spots, dried on food, etc. If there are any, give them a quick shot of all purpose cleaner.

❑ Using a brush or plastic scrubber, scour the electric stove **Drip Pans and Rings** that have been soaking in the sink. Set them next to stove.

❑ Reach your hand in the holes where the drip pans go and clean the ''floor'' of the stove top. Then polish the **Stove Top**, hood and backsplash with all purpose or window cleaner (depending on whether or not the areas are greasy).

❑ Now move to your left or right, working around the room in an orderly manner. Carry your supplies with you. Try not to retrace your steps at all.

❑ **Polish Appliance Surfaces** with glass cleaner and paper towels. Follow specific instructions below for each one:

· **Oven:** Open door(s), wipe window and top of door.

· **Dishwasher:** Wipe the outside, then open the door and wipe inside edges of door.

· **Refrigerator:** Wipe outside (including top!). Open door, wipe the chrome top and rubber gasket, drawer fronts and any obvious spots inside. Clean air vent at the bottom with a quick swipe of the sponge (or canister vacuum if you will be using it on the floor later).

· **Microwave Oven:** Wipe inside and out.

❏ **Clean Counter Tops**, moving and polishing appliances, etc. as you go. (Pull items towards you, clean counter, slide them back, wiping each one as you go.) Check cupboards and drawers for fingerprints.

❏ **Wash Window and Sill** above the sink.

❏ **Clean Sink** with all purpose cleaner (or cleanser if it's porcelain). Use toothbrush around garbage disposer opening and around edges where sink and counter meet.

❏ **Polish Sink Fixtures.** Use toothbrush around faucet and handles plus base of fixture.

❏ **Empty Trash.**

❏ **Sweep or Vacuum Floor** using a sponge in corners and on baseboards as needed.

❏ **Wash Floor** watching for spots that may need special attention. Be sure to rinse sponge or mop often, changing water as needed.

You may wish to use sink to rinse mop instead of a bucket. If so, mop your way out of the door and let floor dry, or use a towel to dry a path from sink to door. Clean sink last.

## The Routine for All Other Rooms

❏ **Start at the doorway** of each room and move around the room to your right or left, carrying your supplies with you. Always, always, always clean and dust from top to bottom. Try never to retrace your steps. As you clean, check for fingerprints and cobwebs, straighten things, fluff pillows, etc. Vacuum your way out the door so as not to leave footprints on the carpet.

❑ Use a feather duster on **Pictures, Hanging Light Fixtures, TV and Stereo equipment,** broad leaf plants and lamps (including lightbulb). Try not to flick the feather duster around any more than need be.

❑ **Polish the TV Screen, Mirrors, Glass-Top Tables** with glass cleaner. It may be necessary to clean the underside of glass tables, too. (If there's a lamp, turn it on to check the glass.) As always, check glass from an angle to be sure there are no streaks.

❑ Move or remove **Decorative Items, Magazines**, etc. from table tops. Dust/polish. Always use two hands when moving fragile or heavy items or those that have two or more pieces (i.e. candle and candlestick). When in doubt, lift rather than slide any item to avoid scratching the surface underneath. Always dust with the grain of the wood.

❑ Move **Books** an inch or so back on shelves, dust shelves and tops of books (dust away from spines). Return books to original position being certain they are nice and straight.

❑ Clean **Telephone** with damp rag–do not spray cleaner directly on phone. Replace hand set, wiping off any fingerprints (like yours, for instance).

❑ **Miniblinds** can be dusted with either a feather duster or dust cloth. Close them and dust them gently from side to side starting at the top and working down. Reverse the slats and repeat the process.

❏ Sweep **Fireplace Hearth** with fireplace broom or use canister vacuum later. A damp cloth or towel may also be used.

## The Grand Finalé

❏ Shake dust mop, feather duster, dust cloth outside.

❏ Put away all cleaning supplies.

❏ Put dirty rags by washing machine.

❏ Empty trash into garbage can.

Now, that wasn't so bad was it? And just look at how the house sparkles, how clean it smells. And it will be even easier (and faster) next time.

## Rotating Jobs

There are some jobs that are not usually necessary to do every week, so we suggest that our housekeepers do one each visit. You may want to add others to the list, but these are the jobs we suggest you do on a rotating basis:

❏ Polish furniture with lemon oil, *Pledge*, etc. Wipe tops of all doorjambs.

❏ Clean outside of kitchen cupboards and drawers.

❏ Dust ceilings, walls, baseboards, and under cupboard overhangs in kitchen and bathrooms. Use a mini-vac, or a broom with a barely damp rag attached by a rubber band.

❏ Using a mini-vac, dust all furniture (including under cushions), draperies, and under sofa and any

other heavy pieces of furniture you are unable to move
during your weekly cleaning.

*I prefer the word 'Homemaker' because 'Housewife' always implies that there may be a wife someplace else.*

Bela Abzug

# 6

## How to Clean Like a Pro

**O**ur clients are often surprised by how much a housekeeper can accomplish in four hours. In large part this is due to talent, study and experience; but the working conditions make a difference, too.

If you were going to hire a professional, how would you get things organized for him or her? Most people straighten the house, get the kids out from underfoot, and so forth. Let's take a look at the situation a housekeeper is likely to encounter. The more nearly you can duplicate these conditions the more you will accomplish during your own cleaning time.

**A professional has a list to work from**. She knows what the priorities are. Decide beforehand exactly what you will accomplish during your cleaning: what are your priorities? Psychologists tell us that if you write these things down the night before, you are far more likely to do them. Also make a list of "extras" to do if time and energy permit.

When cleaning day dawns, wake up saying "I will stick to my list; I will not get sidetracked!" Then if you see magazines that need sorting or a closet that should be reorganized, make a mental note and schedule it for another time—or do it after you've finished everything on the list. Distraction is your number one enemy when cleaning your own home. Set your goals and don't deviate from them.

**A professional doesn't have kids to contend with.** If at all possible, clean your house when there are no little people around. Take them to a sitter, trade with a neighbor, enlist the aid of your husband. Be creative. But don't try to clean and "mother" at the same time.

**A professional isn't interrupted by the telephone.** Take the phone off the hook or vow not to answer it if it rings. Just think, if you weren't home you'd never know the darn thing was even ringing. And life would still go on. Every break in your routine is a time robber. It takes time to stop what you're doing, time to start doing another task, time to complete that task and then more time to start in again on what you were doing in the first place! Interruptions are far more time-consuming than they may seem.

**A professional (usually) starts with a house that's straightened and ready to be cleaned.** Try getting your house picked up the night before. Get all your supplies out, too. Then set that list next to them. It will be a lot easier to begin the next day if everything is ready to go.

**A professional must work within a certain time frame.** Set your own time limit. Try to improve your time a little each week. This will keep you moving and on track.

**A professional is paid for the work.** Okay, so maybe no one is going to pay you for your efforts, but at least you can do something nice for yourself when you're finished. Whether it's a banana split, a great book or a leisurely bubble bath, give yourself a treat.

*My husband and I have figured out a really good system about the housework: neither one of us does it.*

Dottie Archibald

# 7

## "Yes, We Do Windows"

If you really want your house to shine, you've got to have clean windows. What's that you say? You hate doing windows? Well, perhaps that's only because you haven't "seen the light" as to how to do them quickly and easily. If you'd like some suggestions, read on.

❑ Buy a good quality squeegee and learn to use it properly. (Go to a janitorial supply company for both.) Or use top-quality paper towels. Don't use newspaper. Not only is it yikky (black stuff all over your hands) it doesn't do as good a job–no matter what Grandma says.

❑ Spray as little cleaner on the window as you can and still get the surface evenly wet when you wipe it.

❑ Wipe the window until absolutely dry. Check it at an angle to be certain there are no streaks.

❑ Never wash windows in the wind, sun or hot weather unless you want streaks. (The reason: the cleaner will evaporate before you can wipe it off.)

❑ When washing windows inside and out, use vertical strokes on one side, horizontal on the other. This way, if there's a streak or miss you'll know right away which side it's on.

❑ If windows (or mirrors) have a greasy look, try rubbing them with a cloth soaked with rubbing alcohol. The film should vanish with one or two passes of

31

the cloth.

❑ If you use an ammonia solution, don't splash it about. It can strip wax or paint off adjoining surfaces.

❑ Be extremely careful of plexiglass or specially coated windows. They scratch very easily. If using a squeegee, apply very little pressure. There are specially formulated cleaners available at janitorial supply houses.

❑ Are mineral deposits or "water spots" a problem? Use lime and scale remover or ceramic tile cleaner available at a janitorial supply house. Or use *Lysol Toilet Bowl Cleaner.*

**Caution:** These products contain acid. Read and follow label directions carefully. Be especially careful when working on aluminum frame windows. Wear rubber gloves.

❑ There are a number of window washing solutions you can use. Experiment. See which one suits you best.

- Plain lukewarm water. That's right, plain old water will do a very good job if windows aren't too dirty. The advantage: no streaks. If you must do windows in the sun, this is the only thing to use.
- Commercial cleaner–*Windex*, etc.
- ½ cup white vinegar to a quart of cool water.
- ¼ - ½ cup sudsy ammonia to a quart of water.
- Lukewarm water with a few drops of *Sunlight* dishwashing soap. (This is the only brand we know that works; there are probably others.)
- Automotive windshield washer fluid. Does a good job and is cheaper than most supermarket products.
- Special glass cleaner available at glass stores (expensive, but some people think it's worth it).

- Our "Special Brew": ½ cup sudsy ammonia, 1 pint rubbing alcohol, 1 teaspoon *Sunlight* dish-washing detergent. Add enough water to make one gallon.
- If windows are very dirty, a cleaner such as Glass Wax (which has a slight abrasive in it) may be best.

□ An easy way to clean outside windows is to use a strong solution of powdered cleanser (*Ajax, Comet,* etc.) and water. Then rinse thoroughly with the garden hose. Then rinse again. The rinsing is crucial. A sponge mop makes a fairly good applicator. It sure beats climbing up and down a ladder.

*A guilty conscience is the mother of invention.*

Carolyn Wells

# 8

## *The World Beneath Your Feet*

**E**asily a third of the questions we're asked involve floor care. Here are our answers to all the questions we can remember being asked–plus a few.

The secret to a long and shiny life for all your hard surface floors is frequent sweeping. It is the ground-in dirt that scratches and dulls the finish.

Similarly, if you will vacuum your carpets every few days, they will stay clean and new looking. Again, it is the ground-in dirt that does the damage.

If you would like to dramatically reduce the amount of dirt that comes into your house each day, put large mats in all your entryways. This will save you countless hours of vacuuming and floor washing while preserving the floors and carpets. Any rough mat is fine for outside the door as long as it is three to four feet long. Rubber backed inside mats can be purchased at a hardware or janitorial supply store. They come in a variety of sizes and colors.

### Hardwood Floors

❑ There are two types of finishes: *polyurethane* (or the very similar Swedish finish) and *wax finish*.

The best way to determine which kind you have is to find an inconspicuous area (inside a closet, under the sofa, etc.) and scrape a spot with a dull knife. If a waxy substance comes off, you have a waxed finish; if not, it's polyurethane. Another test is to apply some polyurethane to an inconspicuous spot. If it flakes off (give it a couple of weeks to be sure) you have a waxed finish.

❏ The most important principle for hardwood floor care is simply this: Wood and water do not mix! No matter what finish your wood floor has, never pour water onto your floor. Excessive amounts of water may seep between the boards causing them to warp or stain.

❏ *Polyurethane* or *Swedish finish* floors may be damp mopped with any of the following: cold tea, vinegar and water (about ½ cup vinegar to a bucket of water) or a few drops of liquid dish soap to a bucket of water. Remember to keep your mop as dry as possible.

❏ Either liquid buffing wax or a coating of paste wax can be used for *waxed finishes*. The liquid wax is easier to use, but make sure you use one specifically formulated for use on hardwood floors–never use a liquid wax that has a water base! You can apply by hand or rent a buffing machine.

When floor luster begins to dull, simply buff it without wax. After 4 to 6 months of wear, buff with a liquid wax. If dirt build-up appears or if wax starts to discolor, use a combination of liquid cleaner and wax.

❏ When *removing stains* always begin at outer edge and work toward the middle to prevent it from spreading. Most stains on polyurethane floors can be prevented by simply wiping up spills immediately. For waxed floors, most stains can be prevented by keeping floor well waxed and by wiping up spills immediately.

- Dried milk or food stains–Rub spot with damp cloth, rub dry, rewax.
- Standing water stains–rub with number 2 steel wool and rewax.
- Dark spots–Clean area and surrounding area with number 2 steel wool and good floor cleaner or wash area with household vinegar. Allow to remain 3 or 4 minutes, rewax.
- Heel marks–Rub with fine steel wool and good floor cleaner. Wipe dry and polish.
- Animal or diaper stains–Try method recommended for dark spot removal. If that doesn't work, affected area may be refinished.
- Chewing gum, crayon, candle wax–Apply ice until brittle enough to crumble off.
- Cigarette burns–If not too deep, use steel wool. Moisten steel wool with soap and water to increase effectiveness.
- Alcohol Spot–Rub with liquid or paste wax. Rewax area.
- Wax buildup–Strip old wax away, using steel wool to remove all residue, and apply new wax.

❑ When moving heavy furniture over a hardwood floor, slip some socks over the legs to prevent scratching.

❑ Deep scratches will be much less noticeable if filled with polyurethane. A toothpick or nail polish brush (cleaned with polish remover) makes a good applicator. Be careful not to overfill.


## Vinyl Floors

❑ Crayon marks can be removed from vinyl floors with a little silver polish.

❑ Heel marks can be removed with a little tooth-paste on a damp sponge. If that doesn't work, try wiping with kerosene, turpentine or *WD-40*.

❑ Removing road tar can be a "sticky problem" at best, but a shot of *WD-40* will often solve the problem

❑ Has your "no-wax floor" lost it's shine? *Bruce* and *Armstrong* each make products to restore the finish. Check with your hardware store or floor dealer.

❑ Most vinyl manufacturers recommend using only cold water to wash vinyl floors, especially the no-wax type, but *Murphy's Oil Soap* may be used. Follow label instructions.

❑ Scratches may be covered with automobile touch-up paint. Apply with a toothpick or nail polish brush.

## Tile Floors

❑ Some tile floors streak no matter how carefully you rinse them. A quick swish with a large towel will eliminate the problem. (Just step on the towel with both feet and "boogie" around a bit!)

❑ Use a sealer (available at tile or hardware stores) on stone or quarry tile to improve appearance and lower maintenance. You can choose either a satin or high-gloss formula.

## Marble Floors

❑ Wash marble floors with a few drops of dish soap in a bucket of warm water. Dry with a towel.

❑ Apply marble polish or paste wax if necessary.

## Carpeted Floors

❑ Spray traffic areas with *Scotchgard* to help retard soil buildup.

❑ For spills on your synthetic carpeting, pour clean water on the spot. Then lay an old towel on top and stomp like mad. Keep moving the towel to a fresh spot until no more moisture comes through. Repeat as necessary. If the carpet is made of wool, you need to be very careful not to put too much water on at one time. This procedure takes care of the problem 99 percent of the time, unless you're dealing with some tomato-based sauces, mustard or red fruit flavored drinks. These substances should never be allowed within ten feet of a carpeted or upholstered area!

❑ Occasionally, there are spots that mysteriously reappear after shampooing. The usual cause is improper rinsing in previous cleanings. If this is the case, flood with water as above, repeat until spot is (hopefully) gone.

❑ Sometimes the spot is coming up from the padding. You can try cutting out and replacing that patch of pad, but don't bet the rent that it will work.

❑ To neutralize the odor of pet spots, try white wine vinegar, or a commercial product such as *Out! Pet Odor Eliminator.*

❑ If the odor persits, the problem is in the pad. Cut and patch as above.

❑ For a carpet brightener and deodorizer, sprinkle with borax or baking soda (about one cup for a 9'x12' rug). Leave it on for about an hour; vacuum thoroughly. (This will also deodorize your vacuum bag.)

❑ Has heavy furniture put dents in your carpet? Often they can be brought up with a fingernail or plastic hair pick. For stubborn indentations, hold a steam iron a few inches above the carpet, gently lifting as you steam.

*Some people pay a compliment as if they expected a receipt*

Kim Hubbard

# 9

# *The Two Most Important Rooms in the House*

Although we've already covered the basic cleaning procedures for the bathroom and kitchen, you may prefer some of the following methods. Be sure to note the preventive maintenance measures, too. Remember: never work harder than you have to!

## Bathroom

### Ceramic Tile

❑ Soap residue on shower tile and glass doors constitutes a major problem in many homes. There are a number of solutions, but no one is effective in every situation (probably due to differing soap formulations). So if one doesn't work, try another:

- Don't laugh until you try it: Remove soap build-up from tile and glass with lemon oil furniture polish available at hardware stores and most supermarkets. Wipe on lemon oil with a clean, soft rag: let it work awhile, then polish with a dry cloth. Or use a dry paper towel or plastic scrubber if film is severe. The slight oil film that remains will help protect the area from future soap build-up.

- Commercial products such as *Tilex* or *X-14* are effective. Be sure you have adequate ventilation.
- *Shout* or other laundry pre-wash is also satisfactory in many cases. Use as above.
- *Glass Wax* is a liquid cleaner available at some hardware stores. Apply with a cloth, let dry, then wipe off. *Glass Wax* is especially effective on the newer clear-glass shower doors (horror of all horrors).

If previous suggestions for removing soap scum fail, try using fine steel wool (not the kind with soap in it) on DRY tile only. Never use wet steel wool; never use it on wet tile. Be sure to test an inconspicuous area first to be sure it won't scratch the tile. If it does, use a finer grade of steel wool.

❏ To minimize future soap build-up:

- Easiest of all, change brands of soap. From our very limited laboratory experience, *Ivory* soap leaves little or no residue behind. There may well be other brands that work as well. Experiment.
- Use a squeegee or chamois cloth to wipe down the lower potion of the tile and door after each shower (no sense in doing the top part where the water and soap don't hit). This simple procedure will not only prevent soap build-up, but mildew and hard water spots as well.
- Tiles and opaque glass doors may be sprayed with a solution of 2 parts water to 1 part liquid fabric softener.
- Apply a thin coat of wax after thoroughly cleaning the area.

❏ Mildew, though ugly, needn't be a problem.

- Although cleanliness is important, the major

cause of mildew is lack of proper ventillation. So install a fan, open the window or set out dehumidifying crystals (available at your hardware store), which will absorb moisture from the air.

· If you already have mildew on tile surfaces, spray a solution of 1 part bleach to 1 part water. Wait for the mildew to disappear, then rinse **thoroughly**.

· Remember to squeegee or towel dry the area after each shower. Close door or curtain

· Use white vinegar to remove mildew from painted surfaces. If this doesn't take it off, use a weak bleach-water solution (test a spot first). Rinse immediately so as not to damage the paint.

❏ For stains between the tiles, try one or more of the following:

· Spray with a bleach-water solution (see page 11). When grout is white, rinse thoroughly.

· Scrub with denture cream and an old toothbrush.

· Cover stubborn spots with white shoe polish or a white fingernail pencil.

· Apply *Tile Guard*, a special latex which bonds with the grout and whitens and seals the grout in one easy step. It is available from the Joan Cook Housewares catalog. (See page 11 for ordering information.)

· Once the grout is really clean, apply grout sealer. Reapply once a year to keep it virtually maintainance-free. Grout sealer is available in tile stores and some hardware outlets.

**The Sink and Tub**

❏ Light stains can often be removed with a cut lemon.

❑ For rust and other dark stains first try a paste of borax and lemon juice. If that doesn't work, use *Zud*. Follow directions carefully; it is very toxic.

❑ Use a *Dobie* or other plastic scrubber on bathtub ring. Use cleanser only when absolutely necessary. Never use an abrasive on fiberglass.

❑ Use a solution of salt and turpentine to whiten a tub that has yellowed.

❑ Use a special fiberglass cleaner for fiberglass tub or shower stall. It will clean, brighten and retard soap and grime build-up. *Protex Tile and Shower Stall Cleaner* is the best we've found.

❑ If your tub has sliding glass doors, cleaning the tracks can be a real pain. Wrap a rag or paper towel around the end of your toothbrush (the one you clean with) and run it along the tracks. Keep using a fresh spot on your rag or towel until the tracks are clean.

❑ If hard water spots are a problem, try one of these solutions:

- Cover with vinegar-soaked paper towels. Let it set up for an hour or so. Scrub with a dampened plastic scrubber. Put a little cream of tartar on it for greater effectiveness.
- Dip a brush in dishwasher detergent and scrub.
- Use *Lysol Toilet Bowl Cleaner*, but be very careful. Wear rubber gloves. Do not get any on painted or metal surfaces.
- Spots on fixtures or the metal frame around the shower door can be removed with lemon oil. Let it set up, then rub with a *Dobie* pad.
- Regular use of *Showers 'N Stuff* will keep showers, faucets and glass free of stains. Follow directions carefully.

- A coat of wax on your chrome fixtures will help keep them spot-free.
- ❏ Chrome scratched or dull? Here's help:
- Automotive chrome polish is formulated for the tough problems.
- *Bar Tenders Friend* is a powder that makes quick work of any metal polishing.
- Nail polish remover brightens dull chrome.

**Toilet Bowl**

If the toilet bowl does not come clean with regular cleaning, try one or more of these methods:

- Toss in 2-3 denture cleaning tablets.
- Add ¼ cup sodium acid sulfate from the pharmacy. Let stand for 15 minutes, scrub and flush.
- Pour a bucket of water into the bowl. The toilet will flush, but will not fill again. Now attack the stains with powdered cleanser or a pumice stone, depending upon the severity of the problem
- Extra fine steel wool or wet/dry sandpaper may also be used for rust–but gently.

**Mirrors**

❏ Hair Spray can be removed from a mirror with rubbing alcohol.

❏ Foggy mirrors can be prevented in a number of ways:

- At bath time, run an inch or so of cold water before filling the tub with warm water.
- Wipe mirror with glycerine.
- Apply an anti-fog product sold for automobiles.
- Wipe with soapy fingers, dry with a paper towel.

❏ If you failed to take our precautions, blow the fog away with your hair dryer.

# And In the Kitchen

### Counters and Sinks

❏ Clean your porcelain sink the easy way. Put paper towels on the bottom and soak with bleach. Let it work a half hour or so. Voila! A sparkling white sink.

❏ A yellowed sink can be brightened with a mixture of salt and turpentine.

❏ To remove water spots from a stainless steel sink, use rubbing alcohol or white vinegar.

❏ Rust spots can be removed from stainless steel with lighter fluid.

❏ Baking soda paste or liquid cleanser will take spots off your Formica counters or cabinets. Never use powdered cleanser!

❏ Give a lovely luster to your sink and Formica countertops, and reduce maintenance–wipe with furniture polish. A fiberglass cleaner can also be used, but most require that you apply, let dry, then wipe off, all of which is more time-consuming.

❏ For a stainless steel sink, put a few drops of vegetable or olive oil on a cloth and wipe the surfaces. Streaks and spots will disappear and the sink will shine like new. Keep the cloth in a covered container under the sink for quick "spiff-ups."

❏ Scratches or knicks on Formica countertops can be covered with a matching permanent felt-tip marker, automobile touch-up paint or with a crayon melted on a  hot knife blade.

# The Stove Area

❏ To clean sole plates (drip pans) of an electric stove, soak them in a strong solution of *Cascade* or other dishwasher detergent disolved in hot water.

□ If pans are beyond cleaning, you can get most of the gunk off with oven cleaner. Just be advised that the shine will forever be removed. Actually, they will look like satin-finish stainless steel, which is not all that bad.

□ If you line the sole plates with aluminum foil, be very careful that the foil never touches the connector unit. Instant short circuit. Very expensive.

□ Remove the filter from above the stove and run it through the dishwasher periodically. If there's a lot of grease buildup, spray with laundry prewash.

□ Attack those nasty grease splatter spots with concentrated all purpose cleaner and a *Dobie* pad.

□ For really heavy-duty grease, use *Dow Bathroom Cleaner* (with the famous scrubbing bubbles), wipe and rinse.

□ After the wall area is clean, apply a generous coat of paste wax. Subsequent grease spots can be removed with a dry paper towel.

**Oven Cleaning**

□ When something boils over in the oven, immediately cover it with salt. When the oven cools, you can simply brush away the residue and wipe with a damp sponge. To remove burnt-on grease, place a cup of ammonia in the oven overnight. In the morning add the ammonia to a pail of water and clean the area.

□ Be prepared for the next time the casserole boils over by placing a piece of aluminum foil (dull side up) on the bottom of the oven. Be careful the foil doesn't touch the connector unit. Now lay on several smaller pieces, so that when the inevitable occurs, you can just whisk off the top piece, leaving another ready and waiting.

❏ Always spray the oven with as much oven cleaner as possible. After it has set up sufficiently, put newspapers on the bottom to absorb the excess cleaner.

❏ A word of caution: If you get carried away and apply too much cleaner, it may overflow the confines of the oven and drip onto the floor and/or cupboard below. Not a pretty picture.

❏ Another word of caution: Oven cleaners will forever remove the shine from chrome. As you spray, cover the chrome trim with a paper towel or sponge to protect it. Cover heating element, light and thermostat with aluminum foil. Always wear rubber gloves.

❏ Check to see if the oven door comes off or folds down flat. (Why doesn't anyone ever tell you these things?)

❏ Use an old sponge to wipe out the oven—one that you can throw away when the job is finished. Stubborn spots may be removed with steel wool. If that doesn't remove them easily, spray them again with oven cleaner and let it set up for as long as possible. Repeat steel wool routine.

❏ Some people recommend cleaning the oven racks in the bathtub. This doesn't make sense to us because then you have the tub to clean when you're finished. If you don't want to muck up the kitchen sink, take the sprayed racks outside, wipe them down with a steel wool pad, then simply rinse them off with the garden hose.

❏ Have you ever turned your oven on after cleaning it only to have the kitchen fill with fumes? A final rinse with vinegar and water will remove any remaining residue.

❏ If you are fortunate enough to have a self- or continuous-clean oven, you will save yourself a lot of cleaning time. However, you need to follow the manufacturer's instructions to the letter. If you do not have the owner's manual, talk to an appliance dealer who carries the same brand oven as yours.

*Housekeeping ain't no joke.*

Louisa May Alcott
***Little Women***

# 10

## *A Little of This–A Little of That*

**H**ere's a medley of our favorite hints and precautions. Hope they're a hit with you.

### Adhesives

❏ To remove labels, stickers, contact paper or decals from virtually any surface, use a hair dryer to soften the glue. Start at one corner and gently peel back while continuing to blow with the dryer.

❏ Or use a warm iron where practical.

❏ Lighter fluid or *De-Solv-It* (available at a hardware store) will remove any remaining residue.

❏ The adhesive residue from old bathtub decals can be removed with *Pro-Tect Vinyl Cleaner*. Spray it on, let it set up a few hours, scrape spots off with a plastic credit card.

### Barbecue

❏ If you clean the grill with crumpled up aluminum foil, you won't have a brush to wash afterwards.

❏ Or place the grill in a plastic garbage bag, add a strong ammonia solution and close it up overnight. A light scrubbing should be all that's necessary the next morning.

◻ Or spray the grill with oven cleaner.

◻ If you coat the area with nonstick vegetable spray before each use, clean up time will be reduced dramatically.

## Beds

◻ Bed making is easier if you pull all linens up on one side of the bed before moving to the other side.

◻ When changing linens, put all sheets and blankets on at one time, then tuck them all in at the same time rather than individually.

◻ Put a fabric softener sheet between the guest room sheets. It will keep them from getting that faintly musty odor that comes when linens are seldom used. This is also good for the linen closet if sheets are not rotated often.

## Chandeliers

Ah, the many ways to clean a chandelier:

◻ To clean individual prisms, place them in a strainer or fry basket and dunk them several times in a solution of dishwasher detergent and boiling water. Rinse in very hot water and drain in a strainer or on toweling.

◻ Cover the table with a drop cloth and spray the chandelier with 3 parts boiling water to 1 part rubbing alcohol. Let it air dry. (Use distilled water if spots are a problem.)

◻ For chandeliers with larger pieces, fill an appropriate-size pitcher or bottle as above and dip each piece in the container. Air dry.

## Chewing Gum

If you have kids, you probably have had to remove chewing gum from hair, clothes or carpeting at least once. Here are the best ways we know of solving this sticky problem.

❑ Press an ice cube against the gum. It should become brittle and break off.

❑ Spray with a laundry prewash. Let it set up for a minute, then wipe off.

❑ Apply cold cream or peanut butter. Launder or wash as usual.

❑ Most hardware stores carry a product called *De-Solv-it*. Or go to a janitorial supply store and get *Freon Freeze*, a spray. Use each as directed.

❑ Any remaining gum residue can be removed with cleaning solvent or *De-Solv-it*.

## Cobwebs

Has the house taken on the Dracula look? You can get rid of those cobwebs fast.

❑ Suck them up with a mini-vac using the wand only. (Kids like to do it this way.)

❑ Wrap a broom with a slightly damp towel affixed with a rubber band.

❑ Slip an old pillowcase over a broom or dust mop.

❑ Always use downward strokes.

## Crayon

"Crayon art" on your walls?

❑ Rub gently with baking soda and water paste.

❑ Put lighter fluid on a cloth. Wipe the area.

❑ Rub with white toothpaste. Rinse.

❑ Turpentine may be used as a last resort. Spot test first.

## Draperies

Freshen draperies by removing hooks and running the drapes through the dryer set on air fluff. Put in a fabric softener sheet or clean cloth dampened with a bit of pine cleaner or your favorite perfume, if you wish.

## Dusting

❑ Dust cloths  can be made out of soft cotton or wool or nylon stockings.  All of these materials will naturally attract dust.  Keep folding the cloth so that you can use a clean portion each time. Dirty cloths can scratch your furniture.

❑ Use an oil-base polish for oiled furniture, a wax-base polish for waxed furniture.

❑ When polishing carved furniture, lay newspapers down, apply liquid polish (lemon oil is good) with a soft brush.  Hold cloth under to catch drips.

❑ Reduce the amount of dust in the house by changing your furnace filters at least twice a year.

❑ Use a new, inexpensive paintbrush to dust shutters, louvers, ornate furniture, pleated lampshades and knickknacks.

❑ When using *Endust* or furniture polish, always spray the rag, then wipe furniture.

❑ To preserve the finish of fine wood furniture, always dust and polish with the grain of the wood. Do not use a circular motion or dust across the grain of the wood.

## Felt-Tip Pen

If your little Van Gogh has created a felt pen masterpiece on your walls, look out. This one is tough.

❑ Sponge area with automobile brake fluid. Rinse thoroughly.

❑ If that fails, paint the area with white varnish and repaint.

## Fireplace

❑ When cleaning out a fireplace, spray the ashes with water to cut down the "dust." Never vacuum out the ashes. Dispose of the ashes in a covered garbage can. Remember, there's always the possibility of live embers living within those ashes. Use caution. Wash tools.

❑ Remove smoke stains with a scrub brush and TSP (trisodium phosphate), which can be found in paint and hardware stores, or a paste of lemon juice and baking soda–leave on for 20 minutes or so. Go over with a stiff brush.

❑ Brick grout can be scrubbed with denture cream and an old toothbrush. Rinse with clear water.

## Glassware

❑ For sparkling glassware, add ½ cup vinegar to final dishwasher rinse. If washing by hand, add a little vinegar to the wash water.

❑ Remove tiny scratches on glass with toothpaste.

❑ One-half teaspoon orange powdered drink mix added to your regular dishwasher detergent will remove those pesky spots on the glassware.

❑ A couple of denture cleaning tablets in a vase of hot water will clean it beautifully. Leave overnight.

❑ If that's not successful, fill the vase with *Lysol Toilet Bowel Cleaner*. Let it stand overnight, then wash with soap and water.

## Marble

Spots on your marble top table? Try one of these:

❑ Rub with half a lemon dipped in salt. Rinse with soap and water. Dry thoroughly.

❑ Rub with toothpaste.

❑ *Bon Ami* or liquid cleanser may also be used.

❑ Apply marble polish as necessary to restore shine.

## Miniblinds

Miniblinds can be dusted with either a feather duster or dust cloth. Close them and dust gently from side to side starting at the top and working down. Reverse the slats and repeat the process. For heavy-duty cleaning, try one of these methods:

· Mix a batch of *Spic and Span* solution. Close the blinds so that the top surface of each slat faces you. Dip a large sponge in the solution, wring it out thoroughly, and gently wipe the blinds from side to side. Wipe with a clean dry cloth.

· For stubborn build-up, spray an old pair of cotton gloves with *Endust* or all purpose cleaner (if they're greasy) and wipe each slat. Men's socks or a terry mitt will also do the job.

· Or take them down and wash in a bathtub filled with sudsy water, then rinse. Easier yet, take them outside, hose them down, wash with soap and water, then rinse. Rehang fully extended while tapes are still damp to avoid shrinkage or wrinkling.

· Or send them out to be cleaned. (Look under "Venetian Blinds" in the Yellow pages to see if there's a service in your area.)

## Odors

The first thing anyone notices about your home (however unconsciously) is the way it smells.

❏ Add a little baking soda or a cotton ball saturated with your favorite scent (perfume, after shave–or *Pine Sol*??) to your vacuum cleaner bag. As you vacuum, a fresh aroma will fill the house.

❏ Discreetly place a saucer or two of vinegar in the room and cigarette odors will vanish.

❏ Put your favorite perfume on the light bulbs before entertaining.

❏ Sprinkle borax or baking soda on the carpet. Wait an hour or so before vacuuming. You've brightened and deodorized in one step.

❏ Toss some cloves or cinnamon sticks in the self cleaning oven before setting it to clean.

❏ Fool your friends into thinking the house is freshly cleaned by putting a dab of *Pine-Sol* on a cloth and waving it around a bit.

❏ If you like air fresheners, choose a really effective one such as *Ozium*, used in hospitals for years.

## Paintings

❏ When cleaning your pictures, be sure to spray a paper towel with glass cleaner and then clean the glass. Never spray glass cleaner directly on the glass, as it may seep into the art work.

❑ Oil paintings should be cleaned every few months with a soft paintbrush (preferably with natural bristles).

## Pet Hair

❑ Get pet hair off the sofa with a clean sponge dampened with a mixture of one part glycerin to three parts water. Lightly brush the area in one direction and watch the hair disappear. Fresh out of glycerin? Use plain water.

❑ Apply a little glycerin to your vacuum brushes to get hair off floors.

❑ A window squeegee on the end of a screw-type pole can also be used. "Brush" the carpet in one direction.

❑ Lightly mist the area with a 1-5 solution of fabric softener and water. Brush or vacuum. (This will also reduce carpet shocks in the winter.)

## Pet Spots

Are pet odors in your carpeting a problem? Try this method: If the spot is fresh, soak up as much of the urine as possible with a towel or sponge. Apply a mixture of ½ cup salt to a quart of lukewarm water. Sponge in thoroughly. Follow with a solution of one teaspoon ammonia to 1½ cups of water. Sponge in thoroughly. Dry with towels. Brush carpet nap. (Be sure to test these solutions on a concealed portion of the carpet first.) If this method doesn't work, try *Out! Pet Odor Eliminator,* available at hardware stores.

## Rubber Gloves

❑ Make your own rubber gloves last 4-5 times longer by simply turning them wrong side out and painting the finger tips with nail polish. (blow them up like a balloon then gently squeeze. The fingers will pop right out).

❏ Small holes can be repaired with adhesive or other waterproof tape.

## Sponges

❏ Sweeten sour sponges the easy way. Wet and then rub with baking soda. Let it work overnight.

❏ Wash sponges in the top rack of your dishwasher.

❏ Save grungy old sponges for cleaning the oven, bathroom or car.

## Telephone

❏ Clean telephone with a damp rag–do not spray cleaner directly on phone. Replace handset, wiping off any fingerprints (like yours, for instance).

❏ A cotton swab dipped in alcohol or all purpose cleaner can be used to clean the push buttons.

## Time Savers

❏ Some of the fastest, most efficient housekeepers we know wouldn't work without wearing an apron (see chapter 3, *Cleaning Your Home Dirt Cheap*). As you approach each room, put the supplies you need for that room in the apron pockets. You will then have everything you need at your fingertips, thus saving lots of valuable time.

❏ Consider some other uses for the apron: Use one or more pockets for any of the following: a soapy sponge (in a plastic bag) for touch-up work around light switches, doorjambs, etc.; debris and other throw-away stuff; small items that need to be put away in another room.

❑ If you use plastic liners in your wastebaskets, keep a supply of bags and ties in the bottom of the basket under the liner. When you remove the bag, the refills are right there where you need them.

❑ If you have a lot of wiping to do in a room (kitchen counters, for instance), carry an extra sponge in your caddy or apron pocket so you can use it when the first one needs rinsing. This cuts your trips back to the sink in half.

❑ If using a broom to sweep, dampen 1-2 inches on a half sheet of newspaper, press the dampened edge to the floor, and sweep debris into it. Faster and easier to use than a dustpan. This does not work with a dry mop.

❑ Keep touch-up supplies in the bathrooms and kitchen in addition to your supply caddy. Window cleaner, paper towels and perhaps some cleanser and a sponge should do the trick.

❑ Spray your dust pan with furniture polish and the dust will slip right off.

❑ Place plastic lids under metal containers such as shaving cream cans and under-the-sink cleaning products. As the inevitable rust accumulates, the coasters can easily be washed or replaced.

❑ A credit card will quickly remove candle wax, paint spots or any dried-on gunk.

## Toaster

❑ For the toaster that got too close to the bread bag: take that plastic off with either lighter fluid or nail polish remover.

❑ Toasters and other small appliances can sometimes become "stained" from the heat. Silver polish will make them look new again.

## Vacuuming

❑ A small, carry-around vacuum (mini-vac) is one of the greatest cleaning tools ever! Use it for "dusting" upholstery, drapes, blinds. lamps, etc., plus hard surface floors, carpet edges, hard to reach areas and cobwebs.

❑ Attach a long extension cord to your vacuum so that you can vacuum several rooms without replugging the cord.

❑ Electric cords can get in your way while vacuuming and dusting. Screw one or two cup hooks behind wood furniture and loop excess cord over the hook.

❑ Save time when vacuuming by dampening your vacuum brushes with glycerin and water solution. It attracts lint, hair and dust like a magnet. (Glycerin is available at your pharmacy.)

❑ If pins, paper clips or the like are a problem, mount a magnet on the front of your vacuum to catch them before they rattle around and damage the vacuum.

❑ Vacuum under a dresser without moving it by simply removing the bottom drawer. If vacuuming the area is not practical, wipe it out with a damp rag or sponge.

## Vinyl

Never use oil on vinyl. It will make it stiff and hard. Instead:

❑ Clean with mild dishwashing soap and warm water. Rinse.

❑ Rub it with a baking soda paste.

❑ If it's really dirty, wash it with turpentine first, then with mild dishwashing soap and hot water.

## Walls

❑ Avoid streaks when washing walls by starting at the bottom and working upwards.

❑ Use a sponge mop for walls and ceilings then a sponge or rag for the areas that can't be reached with the mop.

❑ An art gum eraser will remove most spots and smudges from wallpaper.

❑ For grease spots on wallpaper, rub gently with cornstarch or baby powder. Brush off after an hour or so.

## Wood

❑ To remove stuck-on paper from a wood surface, apply a small amount of lemon or vegetable oil and remove with a soft cloth. Rub remaining oil into the surface.

❑ Scratches on your furniture? Here's help: For small blemishes try toothpaste—its mild abrasive action is effective on minor scratches. For deeper scratches or wide areas use a blend stick, crayon, liquid shoe polish or paste boot polish. Apply toothpaste to even out the finish after coloring. Then wax with furniture polish and buff with a clean cloth.

❑ Water spots on wood finishes can be removed with any of the following: a little lemon oil applied with your finger, baking soda applied with a cloth-covered damp toothbrush, or a paste of cigarette ashes and mayonnaise (yuck!). As a last resort, try superfine steel wool dipped in mineral oil. Rub gently with the grain of the wood. Rewax.

❏ Cigarette burn on your table? Rub with mayonnaise. Let set for an hour or so, wipe with a soft cloth. Repeat if necessary.

❏ Candle wax on wood finishes can be removed in two ways: soften with a hair dryer, then wipe with paper towels or scrape off with a plastic credit card. Any residue can be taken off with vinegar and water. Dry immediately.

## Precautions

❏ Be very cautious that you have proper ventilation if using mildew cleaners such as *X-14* or *Tilex*. The fumes can cause inflammation of the lungs.

❏ Never–repeat–**NEVER** mix your cleaning chemicals!! The resulting fumes can be deadly.

❏ Never use powdered cleanser on formica, fiberglass, marble, vinyl, chrome or stainless steel as it will scratch these surfaces.

❏ Liquid cleaners and most mildew cleaners contain bleach. Be careful not to get them on carpeting, towels, clothes, etc.

*It is better to have loafed and lost than
never to have loafed at all.*

*James Thurber*
**Fables for Our Time**

# 11

## Out, Out Damned Spot

Shakespeare's Lady Macbeth may have been the first to say it, but all of us have known the frustration of a stain on a favorite dress or in the middle of Great Grandma's embroidered tablecloth. Arghh! But with knowledge, care and persistence, you can wipe out most any spot.

### General Guidelines

Before moving to specific stains and how to treat them, read these guidelines for all stains. They are important.

1. Tackle any stain promptly. Flood a nongreasy stain with club soda to keep it from setting. Sprinkle a greasy stain with an absorbent such as cornstarch or talc, brush off after 10 minutes or so. As soon as possible, take care of any remaining spots using one or more of the methods outlined here.

2. If you don't know what the spot is, follow procedure for "Mystery Stain."

3. Apply stain remover from the wrong side of fabric. Push the spot out, don't rub it in.

4. To prevent a ring, use a cotton swab to apply the cleaning agent to just the outer edge toward the spot and work towards the center. If a ring has already

formed, work from the center and gently feather the cleaner out past the ring.

5. Always air dry the article after stain appears to be out. Some spots will "reappear" when dry. If put in the dryer, the heat will have set the stain precluding further treatment.

6. Work carefully. Follow all fabric care directions. Test any cleaning agent on a hidden portion of the fabric.

7. When using cleaning solvent or other chemicals, follow manufacturer's instructions to the letter.

8. Don't give up! If your first method doesn't work, repeat it or use another one.

## Let's Get Specific

**Baby Food**
- Presoak for several hours in a solution of ½ cup bleach, ½ cup dishwasher detergent (dissolved in hot water) and 1-2 gallons of water. Wash as usual.
- For odor, apply baking soda paste.

**Bleach Spot**
- Permanent felt tip pen.
- Rit dye or food coloring mixed to match.
- A 50-50 vinegar and water solution will set the color.

**Ball Point Pen**
- Spray with cheap hair spray (one with lacquer). Blot with absorbent cloth. Repeat as necessary.
- Rub with white toothpaste. Wash as usual.
- Sponge with nail polish remover. Launder.

**Blood**
- Soak in enzyme presoak and cold water if fresh; warm water if spot has dried.

- Wash area with 1 teaspoon white vinegar in a quart of water, then spot with a cleaning solvent. Do not rub. Launder.
- Soak for 30 minutes in solution of ½ teaspoon liquid dishwasher detergent and 1 teaspoon ammonia in a quart of water. Rinse.
- Thoroughly wet area, sprinkle with meat tenderizer. Wait 1-2 hours. Wash in cold water.
- Peroxide will sometimes remove a fresh stain if bleaching is not a problem.
- *Z'out* or *Simple Green.*

### Butter, Cooking Oil
- Blot with a paper towel.
- Rub on cornmeal to absorb grease. Brush off.
- Apply prewash. Rinse. Wash in hottest water safe for fabric.

### Candle Wax
- Scrape off as much as possible.
- Place towel under spot, paper towels on top and iron the area.
- Keep moving towels to a fresh spot until all wax is absorbed.
- Any residue can be taken off with cleaning solvent.

### Chewing Gum
- Harden gum with ice cubes, scrape off with a dull knife.
- Place face down on paper towels or cloth, sponge with cleaning solvent.

### Chocolate
- Soak in enzyme presoak and cold water.
- Soak in cold water then apply paste of liquid detergent and nonchlorine bleach. Let set for 30 minutes. Launder as usual.
- Apply prewash stain remover and wash.

- If color remains, sponge with a peroxide (spot test first).
- If grease spot remains, use cleaning solvent.

**Coffee or Tea**
- Pour boiling water through back side of stain.
- For delicate fabrics, soak in cold water, then use prewash product.
- Treat coffee with cream as a greasy stain. Sponge with solvent. Rinse.

**Cosmetics**
- If prewash doesn't work, apply a cleaning solvent and gently rub until stain is gone. Rinse.
- Fresh white bread pressed into a ball can sometimes "erase" the stain.

**Crayon**
- Treat as candle wax.
- Apply shortening, then prewash.
- Soak in a solution of 1 cup dishwasher detergent (dissolved in hot water) and 1 cup baking soda in your washing machine. Fill on small load setting with hottest water for fabric. Agitate until spots are gone. This procedure is especially effective when a crayon has gone through the clothes dryer with a load of clothes or a stain is very persistent.
- Soak with turpentine.

**Fruit**
- For tough fabrics, pour boiling water through stain from back side.
- Sponge with white vinegar
- Occasionally cheap hair spray is effective. Saturate stain, rub with fingers. Wash in hottest water safe for fabric.

**Glue**
- Check back of package for manufacturer's cleaning instructions.

- If glue is hard, apply hot wine vinegar until glue is soft, scrape with a dull knife. Wash in hottest water safe for fabric.

**Grass**
- Presoak in cold water at least 30 minutes.
- Apply prewash or liquid detergent. Launder.
- If stain persists, sponge with rubbing alcohol (spot test first).

**Gravy**
- Scrape off excess. Rub with cornmeal. Brush off.
- Apply prewash. Rinse. Wash in hottest water safe for fabric.

**Grease**
- Pretest with prewash, liquid detergent or shampoo. Wash in hottest water safe for fabric.
- Place spot face down on paper toweling. Apply cleaning solvent through back of fabric, rub with clean cloth. Move spot to fresh area of towels, repeat. Launder.
- If washing a whole load of greasy clothes, add a can of cola to the wash water.
- Absorb grease on carpet or upholstery with baking soda or corn starch. Rub area with soft, clean brush. Allow to stand overnight. Vacuum. Remove any residue with clean cloth.

**Lipstick**
- Saturate with cheap hair spray. Wash with detergent.
- Treat with prewash. Launder as usual.
- Rub with cleaning solvent until outline of stain is gone. Wash with hottest water safe for fabric.

**Mattress Spots**
- Flood fresh spot with water, blot with towels. Dry with hair dryer.
- If spot is set, use carpet shampoo or *Out!*.

- Baking soda or *Carpet Fresh* can be rubbed into the spot if any odor remains. Vacuum off.

## Meat Juice
- Presoak in cold water for 30 minutes. Launder with detergent and bleach safe for fabric.

## Mildew
- Very difficult to remove; treat as promptly as possible. Untreated stains can damage fabric beyond repair.
- Rub with prewash, launder in hottest water and bleach safe for fabric.
- If stain remains, sponge with lemon juice and salt.
- Place wet article in sun to dry. Leave it all day, if possible.

## Mud
- Brush off excess and rub with a paste of liquid detergent and nonchlorine bleach.
- Wash with extra detergent.

## Mustard
- Treat promptly, this is a tough stain.
- Run water through back of stain.
- Rub with liquid detergent. Let set for 20 minutes. Wash in hottest water safe for fabric.

## Nail Polish
- Apply polish remover with cotton swab (except on acetate fabrics). Blot with paper towels. Repeat until no polish is picked up on blotter.
- Sponge with a 2-1 solution of denatured alcohol and ammonia. Wash.
- For acetate fabrics, dab with turpentine followed by ammonia. Wash.

## Paint, Latex
- If paint is still wet, remove as much as possible

with a dull knife, flush area with water and rub
with soap or liquid detergent.
- If paint has dried, try rubbing the fabric between
your fingers to break paint into powder. Proceed
as above.

## Paint, Oil Base
- Sponge with paint remover or turpentine.
- Try applying banana oil to old stains, then sponge
with cleaning solvent. Launder as usual.

## Pencil
- Rub with a soft eraser.
- Rub with liquid detergent.
- Sponge with glycerin, then ammonia. Rinse.

## Perspiration
- Sponge fresh stain with ammonia and wash in
hottest water safe for fabric.
- Rub an old stain with white vinegar, wash in the
hottest water safe for fabric.
- Wet stained area, sprinkle with meat tenderizer,
let stand for several hours. Wash as usual.
- Soak garment; expose stained area to all-day sun.
- If odor remains, soak in a salt and water solution.
- For persistent odor, sponge with clear mouth-
wash (spot test first). Launder.

## Rust
- Soak in lemon juice and salt solution. Place wet
garment in sun for the day. Rinse.
- Place stained area face down over boiling water.
Apply lemon juice while steam penetrates fabric.
Repeat as necessary. Rinse.
- Apply a solution of 1 teaspoon oxalic acid crys-
tals in 1 cup water with a cotton swab or sponge.
Use extreme caution: oxalic acid is poisonous.
- Use a commercial rust remover for fabrics. Fol-
low directions carefully.

## Scorch

- Prewash in cold water, apply prewash and launder as usual. Dry in hot sun until stain is gone.
- Soak area with hydrogen peroxide (spot test first). Place on paper toweling, cover with a piece of cotton sheeting (an old pillowcase works fine) and press with a hot iron. Rinse thoroughly.

## Shoe Polish

- Apply prewash or liquid detergent. Rinse. Repeat as necessary. Wash in hottest water safe for fabric.
- Sponge with rubbing alcohol. Rinse and launder.

## Tar

- If soft, scrape off as much as possible with a dull knife, or else soften with Vaseline or shortening.
- Sponge with cleaning solvent or kerosene (spot test first). Apply prewash and launder.

## Urine, Feces and Vomit

- Rinse article in cold water.
- Rub with liquid detergent and treat with enzyme presoak.
- For persistent stain, sponge with white vinegar. Rinse and launder as usual.

## Wine

- Sponge with cold water as quickly as possible.
- Apply glycerine and liquid detergent. Rinse with warm water.
- If spot remains, add a few drops of ammonia to detergent. Sponge area and rinse thoroughly.
- If spot turns pink, white vinegar may be effective.

## The Mystery Stain

There are times—more often than we'd like to admit—when you have absolutely no idea what caused that spot on your favorite dress. You can probably get it out, however, if you will follow these steps:

1. Place the spot face down on a towel, sponge with club soda, mineral water or tap water. Often this is all that's needed for the easy stuff. If the stain remains, proceed.

2. Soak area in cool water for an hour or so. Wring out excess water and gently rub prewash into spot. Let it set up for a few minutes, run cold water through the spot from the wrong side of fabric. If stain remains, repeat several times as necessary.

3. Wash in hottest water safe for fabric. Add appropriate bleach for fabric. Add a little extra detergent.

4. Line dry.

5. If the stain persists, soak again in club soda or water.

6. Turn fabric wrong side out, place it on towels, apply cleaning solvent for maximum time manufacturer suggests (usually five minutes or so). Rinse.

7. If the stain is still visible, you will probably want to consult your dry cleaner. You can, however, repeat the above steps as often as you wish.

*A clean house with untidy closets is like being all dressed up with a dirty neck.*

*Anonymous*

# 12

## *Organizing Behind Closed Doors*

**I**f you have followed our suggestions thus far, no doubt your house positively sparkles. In the next two chapters we'd like to address a distinctly contemporary phenomenon common to most of us in this consumer-oriented society. The problem is clutter with a capital C. Clutter in closets, cupboards and drawers, as well as the everyday stuff on tables, counters and floors.

You move, shuffle, stack and remove it. You argue about it, curse it, cram it and search for it. If ever you are going to get control of this beast we call Housework, the clutter has got to go. But where to start?

## Mental Preparation I

The first step is to prepare yourself mentally for disposing of "excess baggage." Most of us hang on to too many T-H-I-N-G-S: things we might wear, sell, decorate, play with, read, look at, cook with or put things in...someday. Strange, how many of yesterday's "must haves" now clutter our closets. And to what end?

Now is the time to strengthen your resolve. Go

through your entire house and ruthlessly appraise the value (to yourself and your family) of everything in each closet and drawer. Really look at what's there. Ask yourself the tough questions.

For instance, will you ever feel good in that little floral frock that was such a steal at 75% off? (Remember, you never had the right shoes to go with it, and it's still too tight around the waist.) Why not donate it to someone who has the puce pumps to match?

Do you ever do fondue? If not, deep six the pot.

And books. Can we be honest here? How many will you ever read more than once? So keep the reference books, inspirational and special books, then pack up the rest and donate them to the library.

Let your rallying cry be, "If in doubt, throw it out!" Give it away, trade it, burn it or put it out on the front lawn with a ''Free to Good Home'' sign. But don't hang on to all that stuff. Let it go. You can do it. You can!

## Mental Preparation II

If you are yet unmoved, you are surely a hard-core clutter collector (try saying *that* three times fast); a hoarder of the first order. To that end, may we mention three bottom line, nitty-gritty reasons for clearing out the clutter.

**Money in your pocket**. Hold a garage sale, put clothing on consignment in a used clothing store, sell items through a newspaper or supermarket ad. It all adds up to money in your pocket.

**More money in your pocket**. Most people are unaware of how much money the IRS allows you to deduct for itemized charitable contributions. For instance, you can claim $10-85 for a woman's suit, $5-20 for a double bedspread and a working black-and-white TV is worth $50-70 according to tax experts. Ask your accountant for a complete list or check at the library.

**Save valuable time**. Consider all the hours of frustration you will save when you don't have to sort through ten items for every one you want to find. Ah, sweet order.

## You've Gotta Start Somewhere

Now get two or three large boxes for sorting things: one for those items you will sell or give away, another for things which should logically be located elsewhere (you can sort through these things at the end), plus a box (or bag) for the throw-away items.

With your three boxes in hand, start with either the closet which can be cleaned out the fastest and easiest (if you need immediate satisfaction) or the one which bothers you the most. Then, proceed in an orderly manner throughout the house. Promise yourself that you will keep at it until all areas are cleaned, whether that takes two days or three months. Be absolutely merciless about what you throw out. Be certain that every item on every shelf has earned its right to be there. Don't be a victim of your own possessions.

**NOTE:** For those who have skipped the mental preparation, or who suffer from severe emotional attachment to all that ''stuff,'' a fourth sorting box may be necessary. This box is for all those things you know you should part with but can't. When this box is filled, tape it securely, date it, store it in the garage. Six months later, give it away!!

Store your most frequently used items in the most accessible areas, closest to where you will be using them. Put short items at the front of the shelves and taller things at the back. Heavy or cumbersome items should go on lower shelves. Upper shelves are ideal for storing lightweight articles and those that you can get down with one hand, such as trays placed vertically. Whenever possible do not store things other than boxes on the floor.

When storing things in boxes, label them clearly and accurately. If you need a number of boxes, get like-sized ones. Check your grocery store for sturdy produce boxes with lids. You can also purchase cardboard file boxes at any stationery store.

If you have a lot of boxes, code each with a number or letter. List the contents for each box on a separate card and put it nearby for quick reference. This makes locating a particular item much faster and easier.

Facilitate orderliness in bedroom closets by installing an extra shelf or hanging rod, put in hooks, hanging shoe bags, and the like. You can spend hundreds, even thousands, of dollars on closet accessories, but there's also much that can be done with only the most basic materials. Many hardware stores stock a wide variety of storage accessories that require little or no installation.

Lastly, remember the KISS principle (Keep It Simple Stupid). This is not a place for fancy systems.

## An Ounce of Prevention

It is said that an ounce of prevention is worth a pound of cure. Preventing future clutter buildup is simple: just learn to say NO.

❑ Say no to bargains. A bargain is only a bargain if you use it. Would you want the item at full price? If not, chances are you won't enjoy it much no matter how much money you "saved."

❑ Say no to duplications. Not long ago, a woman phoned into one of those TV shopping stations to order a watch. "Oh, I'm so thrilled to get this one," she gushed. "I don't have *any* silver and gold ones." "Oh? And how many watches to you have?" asked the host. "Well," she replied happily, "I had 95, this will make 96. Just four more and I'll have an even 100!"

As collections go, this one's pretty harmless space-wise. But if we're talking "duplications," it's ridiculous.

❑ Say no to impulse buying. Consider each purchase carefully. Is this a "need" or just a momentary "want"? Check your clothes closet. How many impulse items are in the seldom-worn division?

❑ Say no to excessive mail order items. If you've ever purchased anything from a mail order catalog, you probably receive at least 20 other catalogs on a regular basis. How enticing they all are. How easily one can get carried away with ordering; how quickly all judgment is suspended.

Can you picture yourself buying these same items in a store? If they are not what you want, are you willing to spend the necessary time and money to return them?

❑ Say no to specialized gadgets. We wonder how many yogurt makers, electrical vegetable peelers and $300 bread making machines, used but once or twice, now gather dust in cupboards all across America. They look so enticing in the Sunday supplements, but are they worth the space they take?

❑ Say no to giving impractical gifts. If yesterday's gifts are today's clutter, perhaps it's time to evaluate the situation. What is it these gifts say for us? Is there another way to get the message across?

*If life's a bowl of cherries, why am I in the pits?*

Erma Bombeck

# 13

## The War against Clutter

You've weeded out all those excess belongings, and considered ways to prevent future build-up. Now let's focus our attention outward. Beginning with an overall evaluation, let's discuss organizing the remaining essentials and some ways to get the family involved in keeping things neat.

### Evaluate

You can gain a whole new perspective on clutter by examining your house as a stranger might. Go out the front door and come in again, this time as a first time visitor.

Look at all the items on table tops, counters, shelves, and the like. Is each one either decorative or used on a regular basis? If not, put away as many things as you're comfortable with (you should have lots of storage space by now). Immediately, your house will look cleaner and your cleaning time may be reduced by as much as 30%.

Second, observe any problem areas and consider possible solutions. For instance, most families with school-age children find there's a magnetic attraction between school stuff (books, jackets, papers, etc.) and the first table inside the front door. Result? Clutter. But in your role as "first-time visitor," you can no doubt come up with a few creative solutions. Perhaps you could simply lock the front door and thus reroute the bookdroppers, or issue book-parking tickets with appropriate consequences spelled out: or have your child count the number of steps from front door to bedroom. Sweetly asking him or her to walk a mere 26 additional steps doesn't seem so onerous as continually commanding that the books be put away.

## Keep Current

Can you believe the amount of potential clutter that enters your home each day? Stay on top of it or you'll soon be buried.

❑ Sort through the mail daily. Junk the junk mail, file the bills to pay. Designate a file or container for "will read" items.

❑ Stash the newspapers daily; magazines every 4-6 weeks. If there's an article you want to read, cut it out and discard the rest.

❑ Use a big calendar to record all duties, family activities, appointments, club dates, calls to make, birthdays, anniversaries, etc. As soon as you receive a schedule, invitation or appointment, record all pertinent information on the calendar and throw away the accompanying paperwork.

❑ If you have children, designate a box, drawer, file folder, etc., for their papers and artwork. Sort through it at least once a year and keep only those pieces that will be meaningful ten years from now.

❑ Set up a filing system for all your important papers (more about this in a minute). As soon as you receive your new insurance policy, etc., file it.

## Divide and Conquer

Several small spaces are always easier to keep neat than one large one. Consider these subdivisions for starters:

❑ Snap-together plastic boxes, a silverware tray, desk drawer organizer or plastic tackle box can bring new order to your drawers.

❑ Clear plastic boxes in various sizes for shoes, sweaters, etc., are inexpensive, stack easily and, best of all, allow you to see the contents. Sweaters, toys, sewing supplies, scarves, gloves and other accessories are but a few of the uses for these containers.

❑ A shoe bag with clear plastic pockets hung over the back of a door can serve many purposes. In a child's room it could hold small toys that are so easily lost at the bottom of the toy box, or socks and underwear, hair accessories, Barbie dolls, the list goes on and on. You might use such a bag for sewing or craft supplies, accessories or all manner of grooming items in the bathroom.

❑ A fold-out lingerie bag hangs in your closet and neatly takes care of jewelry and/or other accessories.

❑ Hardware and department stores carry all sorts of pretty boxes, plus closet and drawer dividers. And don't forget about plain old shoe boxes, which can be very attractive if covered with wrapping paper.

## Consolidate

For all the remaining clutter, consolidation is probably the best solution. Of course, everyone must have a junk drawer. And a basket or two strategically placed can serve as an "in basket" for those little things you don't have time to put away or don't know where to put. When it's full, clean it out.

The ultimate "consolidator" is undoubtedly the file box or cabinet. A nice looking two-drawer oak file cabinet can be purchased for $100-150 and can serve as a table or telephone stand as well.

Some department stores carry file boxes in a variety of decorative prints. Or you can decorate one to match your decor. You may even have a kitchen drawer that can accommodate file folders. Now go to the stationery store and get a pack of hanging file folders and tabs. Organization looms ahead.

Think of all the important papers you now have scattered around the house: bills to pay, store receipts, product warranties, bank statements, school booklets and papers, insurance policies. Make a file for each. This is also a good place to put magazine articles you have cut out to read, recipes to file, letters to answer, etc.

Imagine all the time and mental energy you will save by having all these important papers in one place. Whatever will you do with all your newfound leisure time?

## Getting the Family Involved

Keeping your house orderly without family cooperation is a little like hanging wallpaper with only one arm. It can be done, but why?

If you have played janitor up until now (because that's what Mother did?) but no longer have the time and/or desire to continue, you can put a stop to it. Your family will cooperate if handled with a little tact and TLC.

A family meeting can be an effective vehicle for communicating your position and creative problem solving. If you start off with a tasty treat such as triple fudge cake with ice cream and chocolate sauce—we all know chocolate is a natural tranquilizer—you are more likely to create a positive, mental attitude in your listeners. After all, no one is going to want to hear what you're going to say.

It's important to remember that—at least in theory —this is a family problem. It therefore needs a family solution. This is no time for a hot harangue or "Oh, me, poor me, what a martyr I am" approach. Remember, no one forced you to play janitor.

It's altogether possible, however, that no matter how loving, tactful, or gentle your approach, you may be met with blank stares or stony silence when you ask for suggestions. It is best, therefore, to be prepared with a few ideas of your own to stimulate the creative juices.

## Some Ideas to Get You Started

❏ Rule #1: "Don't put it down, put it away." (Wouldn't it be great if you could automatically play that message every time the front door was opened?)

❏ Insist that every family member over the age of two put away all their belongings before dinner is served. Be sure to give everyone plenty of time. Be specific as to what you mean by "put away" (out of sight or where it belongs).

❏ Schedule a different family member each night for pickup duty. His or her things must be put away, the others may be put inside the owner's bedroom door for him/her to put away.

❏ Create a "Saturday Box" where everyone's litter is deposited each day. Come Saturday, they may regain possession by doing a chore or paying for each item they take out. Whatever is not claimed after a specified number of weeks is given to the needy.

❏ Set a goal of a certain number of clutter-free days. If that goal is attained, the family earns an outing of some kind. This may be all it takes to break bad habits—at least for awhile!

*Nagging is constructive criticism too
frequently repeated*

Percy Cudlipp

# 14

## *Children's Bedrooms: A Special Case*

In many homes there is a mysterious nether world inhabited by the child of the family. Referred to by their parents variously as The Pit, The Death Trap, or Scuz City, it is generically called A Child's Bedroom. Often the condition of this room is a major cause of disharmony within a family–ranking right up there with "Stop teasing your sister–now!" and "Turn that TV down!"

There are of course two schools of thought on this issue. If you don't firmly subscribe to one or the other, perhaps now is the time to think things through.

Some people generally view a child's bedroom as his or her own private space to be kept to his own standards. If this is your concept, simply shut the door and, more important, "zip your lips." Depending on the occupant's age and mind set, natural consequences will probably force him or her to shovel it out periodically.

On the other hand, there are those parents who feel that as the bedrooms are a part of the family home they should be kept up to family standards.

Quite obviously, there is no right or wrong approach here. But the more resolute your viewpoint, the more successful you will be either in enforcing the rules or ignoring the whole mess.

## Bringing Order Out of Chaos

If, after careful consideration, you've decided that your child's bedroom needs to be brought up to family standards, here are some suggestions for making the job easier for you both. See how they work for you.

- Insist that the room is cleaned up before dinner, TV, story time, weekend activities, or whatever else works.
- Reward a job well done with a star on the chart, a small treat, or with points towards something the child wants. This can be done on a regular basis or by surprise inspections.
- Write a note from time to time telling the child specifically what he/she is doing well. Never underestimate the power of the written word!
- If the room is not straightened before you or a housekeeper cleans the house, the occupant must do all the vacuuming and dusting, emptying the trash, etc., plus the straightening he/she was supposed to do originally.
- Emphasize how good the occupant must feel to have everything orderly and neat, to be able to find everything--or whatever else applies. Acknowledge that this is no easy task, but it certainly helps out the family, makes you proud, keeps the health inspector from the door, et cetera, et cetera. You get the picture.

## "This Kid Has It Easy"

If this is a new program for your children, it is especially important that you start out slowly. Do not overwhelm the poor kid with demands. Add responsibilities slowly, one at a time.

You and your child will both be a lot happier if you make the room as easy as possible to keep neat and orderly. Get down on your knees,–c'mon, it won't hurt you–and look at the world from a child's-eye view. There's a lot you can do to make cleanup and maintenance easier. For starters, you can:

- Lower the clothes rack in the closets.
- Put in plenty of large hooks for play clothes, nightclothes, a backpack, etc.
- Put dividers in drawers.
- Label drawers with words or pictures, so things get put away in the proper space.
- Use several smaller toy containers rather than one large one. With luck, only 25 rather than 50 toys will be dumped on the floor.
- To minimize bed making, use a contoured bottom sheet and a comforter with a removable cover that can be washed. (This works great for grown ups, too.) But, remember, even with this simplification, it's difficult for little people to make a bed.
- Designate one drawer for junk.
- A clear plastic shoe bag hung over a door is a great place to store craft supplies, small toys, rolled up underwear, hair ribbons, etc.

- Use clear storage containers wherever possible. Jars for marbles, little plastic soldiers, felt-tip pens, etc. Plastic shoe boxes and sweater boxes for larger things. What can be seen will not be dumped—maybe.
- Putting a bed on stilts or suspending it from the ceiling gives the child a generous play and storage space underneath.
- Consider rotating toys occasionally. This cuts down on the number to be put away and gives Junior "new" ones to play with when they are brought out of hiding.

## Some Words of Caution

What do you mean when you say, "Clean up your room"? Now, that may sound like a dumb question, but your concept of a clean room may be entirely different from your child's idea. Too often we ask a child to do something—clean up the kitchen, mow the lawn, dust the living room—and then get angry because the finished product doesn't match our mental picture of what it should look like. Spend time demonstrating specifically what needs to be done and how to do it. Babies do not come into this world with an instinctive knowledge of how to make a bed. Teach necessary skills. Assume nothing.

Just one final word: Try to keep things in perspective. Junior's bedroom may make the aftermath of Hurricane Hilda look picturesque by comparison, but how much is it really going to matter ten years from now?  If you had to name the twenty most important things you want to teach your child, where would room cleaning fall?  It's something to consider.

*I hate housework! You make the beds,*
*you do the dishes—and six months later*
*you have to start all over again.*

*Joan Rivers*

# 15

## *Practical Is Not a Dirty Word*

We tell our clients that we can generally clean 1800 to 2200 square feet in four hours. But we've seen houses of 1000 square feet that could never be finished in that length of time, and those of 3000 square feet that you could zip through in four hours flat.

What accounts for these differences? Three things:

**General condition of the house:** How long has it been since it has felt the touch of a dust cloth, the caress of a mop? Is the house picked up, ready to be cleaned?

**The floor plan:** Does one area flow into another or is it cut up into lots of small rooms? Is it all on one level, or two or three? And so forth.

**The design and decoration.** If you've followed the system so far, the general condition of your house is not a problem. And you certainly can't do much about the way the house is laid out. But your choice of decorating materials, colors, textures, etc., can make an enormous difference in the time it takes to clean the house.

You should hear a housekeeper groan about cleaning the black bathtub that fits a family of six or the brass bathroom fixtures that need polishing every week. How about kitchen windows that come right down to the counters thereby catching every splatter of soap or soup? Or the vast collections of perfume bottles, lacquer boxes or crystal figurines (probably set on a shiny mahogany table) that have to be dusted every time. And then there are the floor to ceiling mirrors that sometimes line whole walls: a nightmare!

If you choose to decorate with these items, fine — just be sure you're prepared to pay the price either in terms of the time it takes you to clean them or what you must pay someone else to do it. By decorating wisely, you can easily cut your housecleaning by many hours each week. Consider the following:

## Things to Avoid

- Very dark or light colors, especially in floors and counter tops;
- Dust collectors, such as knickknacks, books, ornate furniture and lampshades, lots of pictures (go for a few large ones rather than a zillion small ones), dust ruffles, etc.;
- Highly textured walls and ceilings; they collect every cobweb and are next to impossible to clean;
- Unfinished wood: once it's soiled, it can't be cleaned;
- Louvered doors and shutters as well as mini-blinds;
- Free-standing appliances (washers, dryers, stoves, etc.). You'll have five surfaces instead of two to keep clean;
- Hard surface flooring of any kind, except in the bathrooms and kitchen;
- Indented or embossed tile or linoleum;
- Clear glass shower doors, brass fixtures that need

polishing (these two together could add an hour per week to your cleaning routine!);
- Glass-top tables, especially where glass is inset into a frame: the crack between frame and glass will catch every crumb and speck of dust;
- Stainless steel sinks if you are in a hard water area.

## Things to Use

- Covers for kitchen appliances to keep off dust and hide fingerprints;
- Glass-enclosed cabinets for collections and knick-knacks;
- Medium colors, patterned surfaces (they don't show the soil);
- Gloss or semigloss paint wherever possible (it's so much easier to clean);
- Dull surfaces: teak rather than mahogany, stainless steel rather than chrome, for instance;
- Area or throw rugs on hard surface floors–they distract the eye from a less-than-perfect floor;
- Baskets or other containers to consolidate clutter;
- Comforters with washable covers instead of top sheet and blankets on all your beds;
- Proper mats on the inside and outside of all entry ways (see chapter 8, "The World Beneath Your Feet").

*The most popular labor-saving device
is still money.*

Phyllis George

# 16

## HELP! (and Where to Find It)

With increasing numbers of women working outside the home, more and more people are choosing to pay for cleaning help rather than spending precious weekend and evening hours doing it themselves. Other people are eyebrow-deep in volunteer activities of one sort or another. Cleaning help is no longer thought of as a luxury; rather it is a near necessity for many.

If you're considering hiring a housekeeper, there are a number of considerations: cost, convenience, personnel competence, reliability. We hope the following is of value.

## Nonprofessional Help

❑ **Hire a student.** Check with a college (or even high school) placement office. Be sure the person has had experience and can give you references to check. You may wish to give them parts of this book to study. Usual charge in our area is $4.50-10.00 per hour, depending on age and experience.

❑ **Barter with a neighbor or friend.** She may be delighted to clean your house in return for a casserole or two, baby-sitting, etc.

❑ **Hire a friend**. It may seem strange at first thought, but it is happening more and more often. You get your house clean, your friend earns some extra money with a job that keeps her close to home and has the flexibility that she may need. If you know someone who loves to clean, this may be the perfect answer for both of you. Just be sure everything is spelled out beforehand. A contract may seem superfluous, but it's a wise idea.

## Professional Help

❑ **Ask friends or acquaintances** if they know someone good.

❑ **Check newspaper ads** under "domestic services." The going rate for independent professionals in our area is $8-12 per hour.

❑ **Hire help through a cleaning company.** There are three basic types of services here:

- Janitorial companies specialize in heavy duty cleaning such as carpet shampooing and wall washing, but generally will do all types of house-cleaning. They usually come out and give an estimate ahead of time; the charges average about $25 per hour in our area.
- Team Services send 2-4 member teams to perform a preset standardized cleaning that never varies. They are in and out in a very short time. Charges usually run between $65 and $80 for the average house.
- Housekeeping agencies usually send one person who can tailor the cleaning to suit your preferences and priorities. They usually use your supplies and equipment. If you use the service at

least every other week, you have the same person each time. Charges average about $12.50 per hour in our area.

## Working with a Housekeeping Firm

There are a number of advantages to working with a cleaning company! You don't have to mess with hiring, firing, reference checking, or dealing with the housekeeper if the job is not satisfactory (unless you choose to do so).

In addition, if your regular person(s) can't come, you can choose to have a substitute. So you are never without service unless you choose to be. On the other hand, if you need to cancel service a time or two, the company can get the housekeeper another job, thus relieving you of those nasty guilt feelings.

The main drawback to using a commercial service is that you may experience more frequent employee turnover. In some instances, you may also pay somewhat more.

*I can live for two months on a good compliment.*

Mark Twain.

*Flattery must be pretty thick before anybody objects to it.*

William Feather
**The Business of Life**

# 17

## How to Get Maximum CPD (Cleaning Per Dollar)

**N**ow here's a subject we really know something about. After working with literally hundreds of housekeepers over the years, it is very clear which situations they're delighted to return to and the situations they dread. You and your housekeeper will both be happier if you follow these simple suggestions.

### What Are Your Expectations?

Be clear in your own mind exactly what your expectations are. What are your preferences? What are your priorities?. Do you want the whole house cleaned, or do you want each room "spring cleaned" no matter how many rooms are completed? Don't assume that everyone washes a floor on their hands and knees–they don't! Don't assume that the linens will automatically be changed–ask for it. Better to assume too little rather than too much!

Write it down! Even if you will be home to show the housekeeper through the house–and we hope you will be—write down specific directions. Indicate what your priorities are and make a list of extras in the event that he/she finishes early. Not only will this clarify your thinking, it will give the housekeeper something to refer to.

Be sure the house is relatively neat, ready to be cleaned. Remember, your housekeeper has no idea what to do with all those loose papers, clean dishes or little odds and ends—and you probably don't want to pay for the time it takes.

On the other hand, some people so abhor picking things up and putting them away that they will gladly pay someone else to do it. If that's the case, be specific about what you want done with clutter—don't make the cleaner guess. We used to work with one housekeeper who would simply collect all the clutter in a room and put it in a grocery sack for the owner to put away. We never heard a word of complaint from her clients, so it must have worked fine.

One further note: if it's toys you want picked up, why not furnish a plastic garden rake for the job? It'll cut time and fatigue by two thirds.

## "Please Do Not Disturb"

Let the housekeeper work without interruption!! The two of you can check the house together at the end, but don't follow her around saying things like "Be sure you do this" or "You missed a spot there." Not only will you drive the housekeeper stark raving mad, but those constant interruptions will slow her/him down considerably.

Similarly, don't get the housekeeper started in the living room then pull her/him to a project in the laundry room, only then to change your mind and request that the beds be changed. Surprisingly enough, it happens like this sometimes—it really does.

If you feel comfortable doing so, leave the house for at least part of the time the housekeeper is there. We have never heard anyone say he or she prefers working when the client is at home. The only exception is where client and housekeeper work together at well-defined tasks.

## Accentuate the Positive

Every once in a while one of our staff members will ask to be taken off an account because "I just never feel like she's pleased with my work."

And yet when we talk with the client she says, "Everything was fine! I never had any complaints." No complaints? Perhaps. But she obviously never had any compliments either. Why not?

On the other hand, that same housekeeper may stay with a really difficult client because "I know she really needs me," or "She always notices the extra things I do."

There is not a one of us that doesn't like to feel successful and needed. There are few of us who do not rise to the level of confidence others have in us. A word of praise only takes a minute. It costs nothing. And it brings out the best in others and ourselves.

So... if you eagerly anticipate coming home to a clean house each week, or love the way your chrome sparkles, or appreciate the housekeeper's dependability, don't keep it to yourself, tell her or him! There are just three rules of praise:
- Be sincere.
- Be specific.

· Put it in writing whenever possible, so that your words may be tucked away and savored again and again.

## Criticize with Care

Of course, constructive criticism may be necessary at times–especially as you and your housekeeper become accustomed to one another. You are paying for a service and it should be done to your absolute satisfaction.

Most of the housekeepers we know appreciate knowing when a customer is unhappy. They want to know where they stand. They want the opportunity to make any necessary changes.

Since part of our job is relaying client complaints (as well as compliments) to our housekeepers, we have lots of experience in this area. We've come up with six principles that should help anyone criticize with care.

· Criticize the behavior, not the person. This should always be the frame of reference, the guiding principle. Refrain from using the word ''you'' whenever possible and the comments will seem much less personal.

· Assume that the housekeeper wants to do a good job. In other words, assume that the imperfection was the exception rather than the rule.

· Be specific. If there were crumbs under the cookie jar and smeary streaks on the stove top, say so. Don't just say ''Clean the kitchen counters and stove top.'' The housekeeper is sure to take offense, because, in fact she did clean them. Such generalities seldom accomplish anything other than putting the worker on the defensive.

- Avoid written criticism whenever possible. It's often difficult to be tactful in writing–especially when you are in a hurry.  Better to tell the housekeeper in person or have him/her call you at work. That way you can present your case and hear the other side too.  There may be circumstances you are not aware of.
- Remember that everyone has an off day from time to time. Illness, fatigue, personal problems all may affect the quality of work.
- Try to always temper your criticism with praise. Point out what was done well along with what you want done differently.  If there's not a lot to praise, and just a few things to criticize, you've either got the wrong housekeeper or you need to carefully examine your expectations.

## When English Is a Second Language

Over the years it has been our distinct pleasure to work with staff members from nearly 20 foreign countries. They have often been highly educated people, a doctor, a lawyer, several teachers and engineers, an executive secretary and so forth; but their lack of English skills precluded their pursuing their former careers in this country.

Although communicating with these folks can sometimes challenge our ingenuity, the positives outweigh the negatives. Without exception, we have found them to be conscientious, willing workers with a better attendance and  longevity record than their American-born counterparts.

As increasing numbers of immigrants and refugees continue to pour into this country, it's possible that at some point you may work with one of the "international set". If so, perhaps you can benefit from what we've learned.

❏ Try to be home the first time. Show the housekeeper through the house, pointing out any unusual features.

❏ Keep your instructions to a minimum.

❏ Speak slowly and clearly, but avoid the temptation to raise your voice or talk down to the individual.

❏ Be sure you are understood. Most of use feel a little embarrassed when we don't understand what someone is saying, and in some cultures it is considered an outright insult to the speaker. So ask, "Do you understand?" Or "Am I making myself clear?"

❏ Provide brief typewritten instruction. Or print them, using standard upper and lower case letters.

❏ Use the most common words for household items: "dining room light" instead of "chandelier," "sofa" instead of "davenport" or "love seat." (If you say "loveseat," and who knows *what* might get cleaned!)

❏ Consider some alternatives to the standard cleaning list. Shut the door if you don't want a room cleaned and perhaps put a "do not clean" sign on the door. Use pictures to illustrate what you want done. Leave the appropriate product next to what you want cleaned, with perhaps an arrow for further clarification. There are lots of ways to get a message across.

❏ Avoid the use of slang or idioms. One of the most difficult things about learning our language, aside from the crazy spelling, is the ubiquitous use of idioms (those expressions that aren't directly translatable).

A funny thing happened to one of out clients a few years ago that serves as a perfect illustration. She left a note for "Maria and Valdez," a bright Peruvian couple with very good English skills. It said, "Jeff's room is a mess. Just do the best you can in there."

And what did this twosome do? Well, they picked up every single piece of clothing and hung it in the closet. All the shoes, books, papers, soda cans and sports equipment indigenous to a teenage boy's rooms were meticulously sorted, stacked and straightened. Every square inch was then vacuumed, dusted and polished. In short, "Maria and Valdez" followed the client's instruction to the letter: they did the "best they could".

We learned a lot about idioms that day.

❑ Keep cleaning products to a minimum. Clearly label the use for anything that is out of the ordinary. Carefully consider products such as oven cleaner, toilet bowl cleaner, powdered cleanser, etc., that are potentially harmful if used incorrectly or on the wrong surfaces.

❑ Check the immigration status. As you know, the Immigration Service has really cracked down on illegal aliens. So if you have hired your housekeeper privately, be sure to check his or her Social Security card and/or green card. Make a note of the number, as you will need it when you fill out the 1099 tax form in January.

*You will do foolish things, but do them with enthusiasm.*

*Colette*

# 18

## *It's All a Matter of Attitude*

Not long ago we came across the following words by one Henry Giles. Since he wrote more than 100 years ago, he addressed his remarks to men only. We've taken the liberty of changing the gender for our purposes here.

> Woman must work. That is certain as the sun. But she may work gratefully.... or she may work as a machine. There is no work so rude, that she may not exalt it; no work so impassive, that she may not breathe life into it; no work so dull, that she may not enliven it.

Take a minute to ponder the implications of those words for all the work you do.

What is your attitude towards housework? The very thought of it makes many a woman shudder. Drudgery ... boredom ... thankless. These are but a few of the words that may spring to mind. On the other hand, in our business we often hear people apologize for liking to clean. "I know you will think I'm crazy ...," they will say, or "I hate to admit it, but ...." It's as if they are confessing to some gross personality aberration.

But, whether you love it or loathe it, there are probably times when your attitude could stand a little adjustment, if not a total transplant. If we can learn to enjoy housework more, chances are we will do it better and faster. Housework may seem dull, but with a little wit and imagination we can enliven it.

❑ **Cleaning is great exercise.** Vigorous housework gives your whole body a workout. If you become conscious of how you are moving, you can work on toning specific muscle groups. It may not replace your regular exercise program, but look at how much you're accomplishing at the same time!

❑ **It can challenge your ingenuity.** Think in terms of time-saving, energy-saving, and money-saving techniques and you'll be amazed at how many new ways of doing things you will come up with. Maybe you'll even write a book!

❑ **You can gain a sense of accomplishment.** Psychologists tell us that one of the major causes of job dissatisfaction in the modern world is that most people are involved in only small segments of any given job or project; they seldom see the whole. Thus, there's little feeling of pride or accomplishment. But whether you clean one room or the whole house, you have accomplished something tangible. You can see the results.

❑ **Housework is a change from the mental to the physical**–a nice change of pace, especially if you sit at a desk all week.

❑ **Cleaning can provide the opportunity for meditation.** Yes, it's true! There is an aspect of yoga called "Housewife's Meditation." This comes about when you are so "into" the task at hand that you almost become a part of it. Anyone can do it with a little practice, and you will find it a refreshing, revitalizing experience.

❑ **You can use your housework time for planning**, thinking through problems, dreaming. With our hectic pace, we never have enough time for thoughts such as these.

You can no doubt add ideas of your own to this list. And that very process will make your cleaning time more enjoyable.  Try it. You'll see.

*Work is the greatest thing in the world,
so we should always have some of it for
tomorrow.*

Don Herold

# 19

## *The Rites of Spring*

**U**nless your weekly maintenance cleaning is exceptionally thorough, there will come a time when a real honest-to-goodness deep cleaning is in order. In other words: Spring Cleaning.

Bear in mind that this could take place at any time of the year. In fact, Fall may be the ideal time. The kids who have wreaked havoc with the place all summer long are back in school. Plus, most people like to do some extra cleaning in preparation for the holidays (which always seem to arrive two to three weeks early.) But no matter when you do it, it will always seem like "Spring Cleaning!"

If you shelled out good money for this book, this is probably not your favorite topic. In truth, it's way down on our list, too. But with housing costs what they are today, it's impractical for most of us to just move every few years rather than tackle a thorough cleaning of the premises.

With a little planning and organization, however, spring cleaning can at least be made tolerable. Just be sure that you make the leap from conceptualization (the planning) to realization (the doing)!

## Organinzing a Spring Clean

❑ Decide what you're going to do. List the tasks by room and/or type.

❑ Set priorities. If spring should turn into fall and you're still not finished, what tasks do you want to have accomplished?

❑ Write a tentative schedule of when you can do what. Be realistic in allotting time for each task. Don't try to accomplish everything in 2-3 exhausting days. Spread it over a couple of weeks with some enjoyable diversions between jobs.

❑ Decide whether or not you will (can) do everything yourself. If not, plan how you will get help, either professional or familial.

❑ Start with a fairly short, satisfying task to get yourself in the proper frame of mind.

❑ Finish each room or task on your list before moving to the next one.

❑ Keep focused on the end result: a fresh, orderly home that will be a pleasure for you and your family.

**One note:** if ever you're going to hire professional cleaning help, this is the time to do it (see chapter 16, "Help! And Where to Find It"). It's amazing how much can be accomplished in eight hours (or even four) of concentrated, organized cleaning. With the following check list you can easily make a detailed plan of what needs to be done. You may want to work right along with the housekeeper. If so, be sure you each have a list of well-defined tasks. (It's best if you work in separate rooms.) Be sure you have duplicate supplies if necessary. Let your helper work without interruption as much as possible: you'll both get more accomplished.

## The Spring-Clean Checklist

You may be doing many of these things on a regular basis, but we've tried to make the list as inclusive as possible. If you feel somewhat overwhelmed as you read it, you're not alone–we felt exhausted just writing it. Do not, however, give up. Decide what's most important, then do what you can. You don't have to do it all this year!

**WARNING: Do not read this material on an empty stomach or while under unusual stress. If you experience dizziness, severe depression or excessive fatigue, take two aspirin and call a friend immediately. If symptoms persist, call a professional.**

_____Remove cobwebs not only in the corners and on the ceiling, but also behind seldom-moved furniture and appliances, inside of cupboards and closets, between plant leaves, under chairs and tables, on dried arrangements, in lampshades and on light fixtures, and the like.

_____Clean fireplace(s) and tools. Wash bricks and hearth as necessary.

_____Remove everything from counters, bookshelves, etc. Wipe each piece and clean underneath.

_____Vacuum inside of closets, dust and straighten shelves.

_____Move all heavy furniture, vacuum underneath.

_____Sweep or use canister vacuum hose on carpet edges and baseboards.

_____ Wipe off light switch and electrical outlet plates.

_____ Wash spots off walls and woodwork.

_____ Remove all pictures from walls. Dust walls, clean picture glass.

_____ Clean light fixtures and bulbs.

_____ Wash windows inside and out plus sash around windows.

_____ Clean inside of refrigerator and oven, dishwasher and trash compactor.

_____ Remove cooktop and clean.

_____ Clean filter unit and fan above stove.

_____ Clean washer and dryer inside and out. Remove lint trap from dryer and vacuum or wipe out the area underneath. (Accumulated lint can be a fire hazard.)

_____ Clean outside of all cupboards, dressers, other wood surfaces. Oil or wax if desired.

_____ Wash miniblinds, shutters.

_____ Wipe out inside of kitchen drawers and cupboards.

_____ Clean sliding door tracks.

_____ Wash off telephone(s).

_____ Dust or wash houseplant leaves.

_____ Dust backs of all large appliances, sound equipment and television set(s).

_____ Remove and clean all furnace vent covers.

_____ Clean radiators.

_____ Vacuum draperies and curtains or run them through air cycle of dryer. Wash curtain rods.

_____ Turn mattresses over and end for end.

_____ Clean (or have cleaned) carpets, draperies, upholstery, bedspreads, blankets, etc.

*His sole concern with work was considering how he might best avoid it.*

Anatole France
**Revolt of the Angels**

# 20

## *And in Conclusion*

**H**ousework may never be painless, but we sincerely hope that it won't hurt quite so much as a result of our words here. Of course, "knowing", and "doing" are two different things. Our own homes are far from models of order, cleanliness, and efficiency. (We know people who have homes like that, but we try not to hold it against them.) And there are a lot of things we consider of greater importance than an immaculate house. There's no doubt, however, that a reasonably clean, orderly house enhances the quality of life for those therein. To that end, we wish you much success.

## Share Your Thoughts

If you found *Dirt Busters* helpful, won't you drop us a line? We'd love to hear from you. You can write us c/o Peters and Thornton Publishers; the address is on the next page. Also, if you have household hints you'd like to share for possible inclusion in future editions, include those, too. If we use them, we will send you a complimentary copy of the new edition when published.

# *How to Order Additional Copies of* **Dirt Busters**

Now that you see just how easy it is to save hours of house cleaning time each week, why not share the good news with your friends and relatives?

**Dirt Busters** makes an ideal gift for Mother's Day, Christmas, birthdays or just to say you care.

To order, simply use the form below. Send it to:

**Peters and Thornton Publishers**
**3483 Golden Gate Way**
**Suite 216A**
**Lafayette, California 94549**

Yes! Please send me_____copies of **Dirt Busters** at $7.95 each.

Please add $2.00 postage and handling for one book, $1.00 for each additional book.

California residents add 7¼% sales tax for each book sent to a California address.

Name_____

Address_____

City_____State_____ Zip_____

Please allow 4-6 weeks for delivery.

# INDEX